Frank O. Gehry   Guggenheim Museum Bilbao

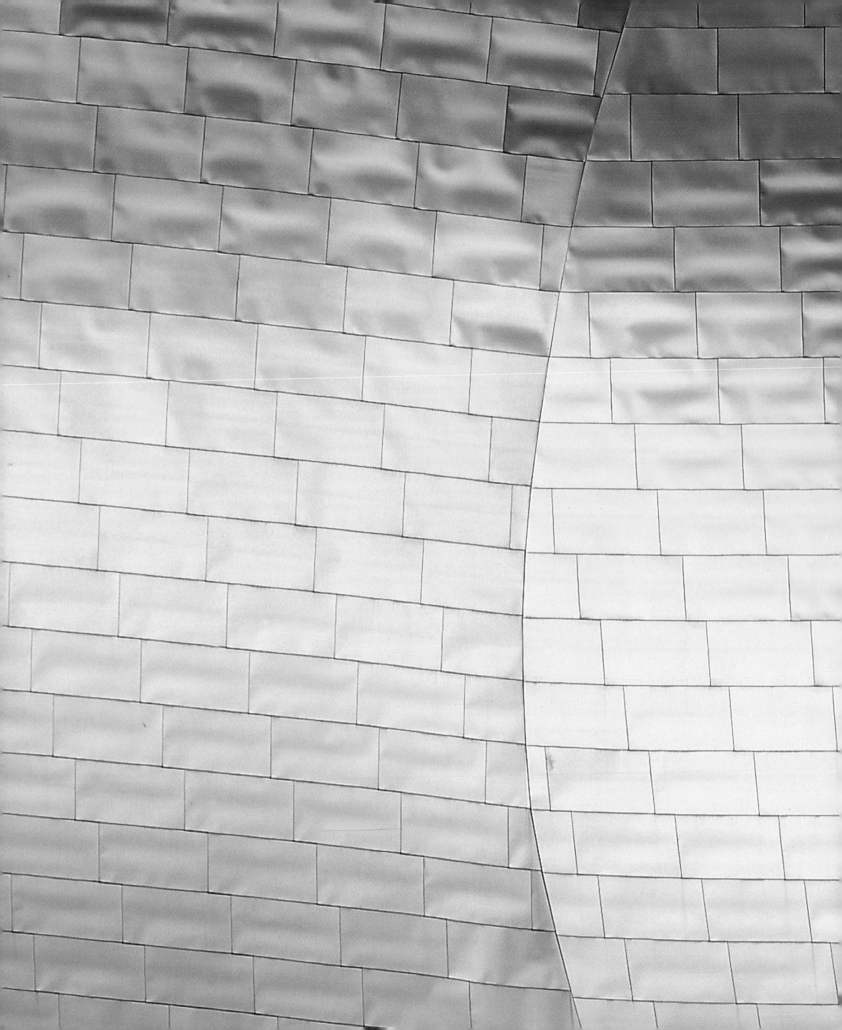

Frank O. Gehry Guggenheim Museum Bilbao

BY COOSJE VAN BRUGGEN

ISBN (hardcover) 0-8109-6907-6
ISBN (softcover) 0-89207-192-3

Printed in Germany by Cantz

Guggenheim Museum Publications
1071 Fifth Avenue
New York, New York 10128

Design: Bruce Mau with Yoshiki Waterhouse

Front cover: Exterior of the Guggenheim Museum Bilbao, seen from the Alameda de Mazarredo. Photo by David Heald.
Back cover: Exterior of the museum and the Puente de la Salve. Photo by Timothy Hursley.

Photo credits (by page): 2–3, Timothy Hursley; 7, David Heald; 8, Aitor Ortiz; 14, Harvey Spector; 16, 19–20, courtesy of Frank O. Gehry & Associates; 23, Harvey Spector; 24–25, Edwin Chan; 30, 32, Harvey Spector; 33, courtesy of Frank O. Gehry & Associates; 35, 38–41, Harvey Spector; 42–44, courtesy of Frank O. Gehry & Associates; 45, Walker Art Center, Minneapolis; 46–47, courtesy of Frank O. Gehry & Associates; 48, Y. Futagawa, ©GA Photographers; 50 (bottom)–54, Harvey Spector; 55, ©1997 Don F. Wong; 56, Y. Futagawa, ©GA Photographers; 58, ©Richard Bryant; 59, ©Peter Mauss/Esto; 60 (left), ©Mark Darley/Esto; 61–63, Harvey Spector; 64, ©1997 Don F. Wong; 65–70, Harvey Spector; 73–76, courtesy of Frank O. Gehry & Associates; 78–79, Harvey Spector; 80, courtesy of Frank O. Gehry & Associates; 84–91, Harvey Spector; 94, 97, Joshua White; 98, 101–02, Harvey Spector; 104–05, Joshua White; 106–08, 110–11, Harvey Spector; 113 (left), ©1997 The Museum of Modern Art, New York; 113 (center, right), Timothy Hursley; 116, Atilio Maranzano; 117, Timothy Hursley; 118, ©Christian Richters Fotograf; 119, Timothy Hursley; 120–21 (models), Joshua White; 120–21 (interiors), Timothy Hursley; 123, David Heald; 124–25, 127–29 (except upper right, 129), Joshua White; 129 (upper right), David Heald; 131, 140, Timothy Hursley; 142–44 (left), 145 (left, center), Joshua White; 145 (right), Timothy Hursley; 146 (right), 147 (left, right), Joshua White; 154–55, David Heald; 156–63, Aitor Ortiz; 164–65, David Heald; 166–67, Timothy Hursley; 168–73, David Heald; 174–79, Timothy Hursley; 180, David Heald; 181–83, Timothy Hursley; 184–91, David Heald; 193, Timothy Hursley; 194–205, David Heald.

Installations: 198–99, The long gallery, with Richard Serra's *Snake*, June 1997; 200–03, Galleries during the exhibition *The Guggenheim Museums and the Art of This Century*, November 1997; 205, Gallery dedicated to art by Anselm Kiefer, November 1997.

Preface

Thomas Krens

Perhaps more than any other art institution in the world, the Guggenheim understands the power of a single building to define its image. Frank Lloyd Wright's landmark Solomon R. Guggenheim Museum in New York is recognized universally as an architectural icon of the modern era, and, since its opening in 1959, has become synonymous in the public mind with the name Guggenheim. And yet, the Wright building is only one of many spaces that the Solomon R. Guggenheim Foundation has occupied since its founding in 1937. It has exhibited the masterpieces from its permanent collection in many homes, including a former car show-room in midtown Manhattan and a Fifth Avenue townhouse that was later demolished to make way for the present Wright building. Since 1976, the Guggenheim has also encom-passed the Peggy Guggenheim Collection, an eighteenth-century palazzo on Venice's Grand Canal, and, for the past five years, the Guggenheim Museum SoHo, designed by Arata Isozaki; in November 1997, the Deutsche Guggenheim Berlin, designed by Richard Gluckman, will open on Unter den Linden, a spectacular location in a revitalized Berlin.

With Frank Gehry's Guggenheim Museum Bilbao, a new star shines brightly in the Guggen-heim constellation. The museum has already been hailed by the world's leading architects and architectural critics as a profoundly important and visionary building. A museum for the twenty-first century, it perfectly complements our New York City base.

In April 1991, I invited Gehry to Bilbao in response to a proposal by the Basque Administra-tion to embark on an unprecedented cultural partnership with the Solomon R. Guggenheim Foundation. As it turned out, Gehry won the competition to design the new museum; I could scarcely have imagined the building that would be unveiled to the public in October 1997. Perhaps every client in the position to award a choice commission and guide its development secretly prays that the chosen architect will reward that confidence with the "greatest" build-ing of his or her career. In this case, we — the Guggenheim Foundation, the Basque Adminis-tration, and the people of Bilbao — enjoy the tremendously good fortune to have elicited from Gehry his best work.

This book celebrates the Guggenheim Museum Bilbao, and reveals the design process that is an intrinsic part of Gehry's revolutionary approach to architecture. Gehry's use of non-traditional materials and his sensitivity to the environments for his buildings are legendary; his method of envisioning a building through semiautomatic drawings and handmade models is little known, but provides the most immediate entry into his creative process.

We are most fortunate to have in Coosje van Bruggen an author uniquely qualified to document the history of the museum, from conception through design and construction. An art historian and artist, van Bruggen has a longstanding relationship with the architect. Not only have they collaborated on various architectural and art projects, but van Bruggen contributed an important essay to the catalogue accompanying the Walker Art Center's 1986 exhibition devoted to Gehry. She has conducted several interviews with the architect over the past six years, and has made a detailed study of his drawings and models. In fact, this book is the first to give Gehry's drawings the prominence they deserve.

I am grateful as well to Bruce Mau Design for collaborating on this publication. Bruce Mau and his colleague, Yoshiki Waterhouse, have sensitively handled the myriad visual elements of this book, bringing them together in a lucid and striking manner.

The Guggenheim Museum's Publications Department in New York guided this book from conception through completion with great care and diligence. For their roles in publishing this volume, I thank Anthony Calnek, Director of Publications; Elizabeth Levy, Managing Editor/Manager of Foreign Editions; Jennifer Knox White, Associate Editor; Carol Fitzgerald, Assistant Editor; and Melissa Secondino, Production Assistant. I am also grateful to David Heald, Manager of Photographic Services, for his important contribution. I would also like to acknowledge those members of the new publications staff in Bilbao who aided in this effort.

And, especially, I thank Frank Gehry for allowing us to reproduce the fascinating design materials that document the process leading up to the Guggenheim Museum Bilbao. He and the staff of his studio — especially Keith Mendenhall and Josh White — have been extremely generous with their time and resources. The resulting book contains a wealth of drawings and photographs that will be as useful to the student of architecture as it will be of value to those who visit this extraordinary building.

New York, October 1997

Preface

Juan Ignacio Vidarte

It has now been more than five years since I was given the responsibility of launching a project that involved as one of its foremost goals the construction of a unique building. We wanted this building to be of the same quality as its contents, with an importance equal to that of the artworks it would eventually house. Over these years, I have been pleased, and to a certain extent astonished, to see the actual project exceeding our ambitions.

From my privileged position, I have witnessed Frank Gehry's building increasingly capturing widespread attention and admiration, both local and international, starting with the first phases of construction. The development of the building has both surprised and moved those of us who have been closely involved with the project. First, the magnificent steel structure, with its tangled design, gave the building its shape; then, fragmented volumes were juxtaposed with regular forms to produce complex patterns; and finally, with the audacious combination of limestone, titanium, and glass, the museum arrived at its definitive appearance.

Today, this building is a reality that stands imposingly in the center of Bilbao's cultural triangle. After so much hard work, it will soon acquire autonomy from builders and technicians as the public and artists take over. Whenever I pause to think that it will outlive its creators, its time—the twentieth century—and all of us alive today, I feel enormously proud of this titanic legacy to future generations.

This project has been a tremendous professional challenge, and its successful completion is due to the enthusiastic participation of a fabulous team. The experience has been of immeasurable value to me personally, since over the years it has allowed me the opportunity to get to know Frank Gehry, a man whose captivating personality is graced with touches of both genius and modesty. It has also been a pleasure to collaborate with the architects, engineers, and other professionals and workers in various fields who have brought to fruition a scheme that only sixty months ago seemed utterly impossible.

Were we to have relied on mere technological effort, however, we would have been left with an impersonal, dull, and anonymous building. Instead, Gehry's architectural masterpiece is the result of the passion that all of us have put into it. It is thus my belief that something from very deep inside us all lies buried within the walls of the Guggenheim Museum Bilbao.

Bilbao, October 1997

Guggenheim Museum Bilbao, plan, July 1991.
Colored pencil and pencil on tracing paper, 50.8 x 82.6 cm.

Passages into the Guggenheim Museum Bilbao

Coosje van Bruggen

Now, in all memories, a fictitious past occupies the place of any other. We know nothing about it with any certainty, not even that it is false.[1]

Jorge Luis Borges

On the verge of completion, the Guggenheim Museum Bilbao has already become an excavation site for researchers digging out plausible truths. The analysis of a building about to be finished may seem premature; yet some evidence of the design process has already been lost, due not only to the selective memory of the architect, but also to his method of moving on various parts of the project at once. Even if writing a case history of the museum requires a certain reliance on the varying recollections of those involved, each from their own vantage point, the building itself embodies its own sources, factual and mythical, to be deciphered infinitely. And that seems to suit Frank Owen Gehry just fine. Gehry feels that his main contribution to the practice of architecture is the direct implementation of an image or form he is in search of. It is this unique hand-to-eye coordination, a process of transforming intact a sketch into a model into a building, that comprises the building.

Exterior and interior views of the Alhóndiga, the site initially proposed to house a new museum for Bilbao.

Preludes, Preconceptions, and the Proposal of a New Site

In early 1991, the Basque Administration was planning to convert a former wine-storage warehouse called the Alhóndiga into a cultural facility. Built early in the century, the Alhóndiga was one of the first cast-concrete structures built in Spain, but is now a near ruin; 28,000 square meters in area, it covers an entire block along Bilbao's Alameda de Recalde, an avenue running toward the Nervión River. Financial resources had been allotted toward its reconstruction, and an architectural model existed by the time Thomas Krens, the director of the Solomon R. Guggenheim Foundation, saw the building on his first trip to Bilbao, on April 9, 1991. He recalled: "They planned to leave the exterior skirt, you might call it, which was a kind of fenestrated medieval castle, and just destroy the whole interior of the building."[2] A high glass box, roughly square, would fit inside the remaining exterior.

Krens was accompanied by Carmen Giménez, the Guggenheim's Curator of Twentieth-Century Art and the former Director of National Exhibitions for the Government of Spain. In the six months prior to their arrival in Bilbao, she had introduced him to a small group he characterized as "influential advisors," including a Basque representative. Several lunches and dinners had taken place in Madrid, at which Krens had presented his concept of an "internationally expanding Guggenheim." At the time, plans were in place for a new Guggenheim museum to be built in Salzburg, Austria; designed by the Austrian architect Hans Hollein, it would be partly embedded into a mountainous site. Because this proposal was stalled, Krens was more receptive to the Basque Administration's proposal to bring in the Solomon R. Guggenheim Foundation as a partner in their museum project.

One can think of reasons why the Basque group would want the Guggenheim as a partner. Since the latter part of the nineteenth century, Bilbao had been a bustling industrial and mercantile community, but in recent times, in the face of recession, it has been in the difficult position of making a transition to high-service industries. Major resources have been devoted to urban renewal: The airport, undergoing expansion, will have a new terminal designed by the Valencian architect Santiago Calatrava; a new control tower by the same architect is already completed, as is a suspension bridge for pedestrians over the Nervión River. While the Intermodal Station Project, started a decade ago by the firm of James Stirling, Michael Wilford and Associates, is yet to be built, the first phase of the subway designed by the British architect Sir Norman Foster is finished. Both projects not only will facilitate travel, but will engender new office spaces, public plazas, and green areas in the city. The conversion of the abandoned Alhóndiga, a remnant of early twentieth-century industrialism, into a cultural facility for the exhibition of contemporary art, would fit within the plans of upgrading the city. But the Basques did not have an internationally renowned collection to put on view in the new museum, nor did they have the expertise to run it. There the Guggenheim Foundation could fulfill a vital role.

On the other hand, why Krens was not put off by this out-of-the-way cultural venue is more puzzling. The answer lies partially in his vision of what a museum can be in our time: "Museums are an eighteenth-century idea, which is the idea of the encyclopedia, in a nineteenth-century box — the extended palace — which more or less fulfilled its structural destiny some time in the twentieth century.... The eighteenth-century idea/nineteenth-century-box concept was predicated on a horse-and-buggy culture where people lived in a region and therefore they came to the center, the museum.... Since people were fundamentally nonmobile, the idea was to replicate the image of the museum as encyclopedia in each location that decided to do this." He pointed out that this kind of institution does not have the capacity to meet the cultural requirements of today, and that even relatively recent museums, such as the Guggenheim and the Museum of Modern Art, New York, have to cope with many problems, foremost of which is space: their art collections are far more extensive than they are able to show. Furthermore, due to the complex nature and large scale of contemporary art, the spaces allocated by museums built even as recently as the Solomon R. Guggenheim Museum — which opened in 1959 — are insufficient. Krens queried, "Is the size of the box a function of the validity of its endeavor?" Pondering solutions to these problems, he came up with the following:

"With contemporary society and transportation being what it is, the idea that the museum does not have to be in the center of the universe to have a valid program also leads to the argument that if the art is significant, people will come to see it, make a pilgrimage to it. And therefore it also makes the argument for concentration. You can afford to get different identities because you're no longer bounded by the concept of the encyclopedia.... A museum can be located in an old textile factory in Massachusetts [the site of the Massachusetts Museum of Contemporary Art] because it has extraordinary space, something that you may not ever be able to enjoy in New York; it can allow for an installation to be put in place and perhaps not moved for a long time, an installation in large scale."

Asked by the Basque Administration what recommendations he would make for the architectural development of the Alhóndiga, Krens's first thought was "maybe not to build this glass cube but to just try to restore the building." The interior space presented a problem, as it was regimented by rows upon rows of columns with no more than 3 meter intervals between each other. The low ceilings — only about 3.5 meters high — constituted another hindrance. Giménez suggested that the parking garage across the street, which had a ramp going up several stories, might better serve as a museum, since it offered possibilities for large unobstructed gallery spaces with much higher ceilings. Although Krens did not want to give up on the project, he continued to doubt that either building, separate or together, could work as a site. He decided to get another opinion, and so asked the Los Angeles architect Frank Gehry to come to Bilbao.

Krens's choice was a natural one. In October 1988, he had engaged Frank O. Gehry and Associates; Venturi, Rauch and Scott Brown; and other architects to develop a master plan and feasibility study for the conversion of the former Sprague Technologies, a twenty-eight-building factory with rough interior spaces in North Adams, Massachusetts — once a thriving mill town, but today a depressed area — into the Massachusetts Museum of Contemporary Art (MASS MoCA). The complex, which will open in 1998, was intended to be the world's

Exterior view of the Temporary Contemporary, Los Angeles.

largest museum of contemporary art and architecture. Although its focus has changed to some extent, and its governing body is entirely independent, MASS MoCA is another element in Krens's vision of an extended Guggenheim.

Gehry is well known for his transformation of industrial spaces. For example, the Los Angeles Museum of Contemporary Art (MOCA) commissioned Gehry to transform 15,400 square meters of warehouse spaces in the city's Little Tokyo section into large exhibition galleries for oversized works in all mediums — from design, architecture, and art to video — as well as spaces for dance and music performances. The so-called Temporary Contemporary was meant to stay open for just three years, until the completion of the museum's new permanent building, designed by Arata Isozaki, located on Bunker Hill in downtown Los Angeles.

The design phase for the Temporary Contemporary was begun during the summer of 1982 and the building completed in November 1983. Gehry began to work with materials he found on the site: the steel girders with redwood decking were fireproofed and left exposed; raw concrete floors were painted gray. Artificial and natural lighting were combined through industrial wire-glass skylights and clerestory windows illuminating the gallery interiors. A series of ramps made the entire building accessible for the handicapped. Gehry chose corrugated steel as material for the loading dock, and accentuated the entrance to the building with a steel-and-mesh canopy spanning Central Avenue, which the city and local community permitted him to close off. In a review in the *New York Times* on November 20, 1983, John Russell wrote: "For the seasoned visitor, the fascination of the Temporary Contemporary lies in the fact that although the rehabilitated building is a model of offhand sophistication, it is in an area that is completely disassociated from high culture." The Temporary Contemporary — now called the Geffen Contemporary — proved so successful that it has remained open even though the Isozaki building has long since been built. Over the last decade, this type of museum — in the form of a large warehouse space with high ceilings — has proven to be one of the better solutions for exhibiting the art of today. Krens knew that if there would be any chance of successfully transforming the Alhóndiga into a museum, Gehry would be the one to pull it off.

On May 20, 1991, Gehry came to Bilbao and took a good look. His immediate reaction, along lines similar to Krens's, was that the Alhóndiga was an unworkable proposition for a museum. He felt that it might be better to refurbish the warehouse as a hotel with places to shop, while retaining the existing structure. Tearing down the exterior would destroy the fabric of that particular area of the city; preserving the outer shell for the new building would result in a discord of scale and style. "My advice was to move the Museum somewhere else," Gehry recollected in an interview in 1995. When questioned by the Basques as to which location he would pick, he recalled responding, "'By the river'...because they had been telling me all day that the river is being redeveloped.... I liked the site because it went under the bridge." Asked in the interview if he actually decided the site of the competition, he replied, "That is correct. It is near the Bellas Artes School, and we started to speculate on a potential connection."[3]

Krens related his visit with Gehry to the Alhóndiga as follows: "Despite the fact that there was a big space and you could walk in the top of this building at nine o'clock at night — it was almost summer time and it was as clear as day looking all around — I think we both came to the conclusion, reluctantly, that it wasn't going to work. And that was no big surprise to me. So Frank left and I prepared to leave later that day. And we more or less told the Basques it was not possible."

But obviously this was not the end of the story. When, in November 1996, Gehry once more talked about the event, he said: "Well, that evening [May 20] before dinner we went up to the top of the hillside, across the river, because it was still light out. And the Basques showed Krens and me the city, and they pointed out the Alhóndiga, and I remember pointing at several sites from above, and saying, 'the riverfront is more exciting,' and then I said that again that night at dinner. Anyway, Tom did a run the next morning, and we went from here across the bridge, down to here, and then back. Then he realized that this was the cultural center. I think it was a joint finding, but he finalized it."[4]

In February 1997, when asked how the waterfront had come into play, Krens answered: "At some point, when it was becoming clear that the Alhóndiga was not going to work as a site and we had already resigned ourselves to leaving the project, there was this moment when I had this epiphany and the epiphany was the function of the famous run through the city, whether it was morning or evening I can't remember. But I was staying at a hotel that was over here called the López de Haro. And I went past the Bellas Artes Museum and then crossed this bridge to the university — and the museum is now located right here. I ran down to the opera house [Teatro Arriaga] and then back to the Bellas Artes Museum and then I realized that this was, in fact, what I called the geocultural triangle of Bilbao. The fact that the waterfront was in the middle of it at this point was only coincidental because it was an open area if you went there, but these were the three major cultural facilities: the Bellas Artes Museum, the university, and the opera house."

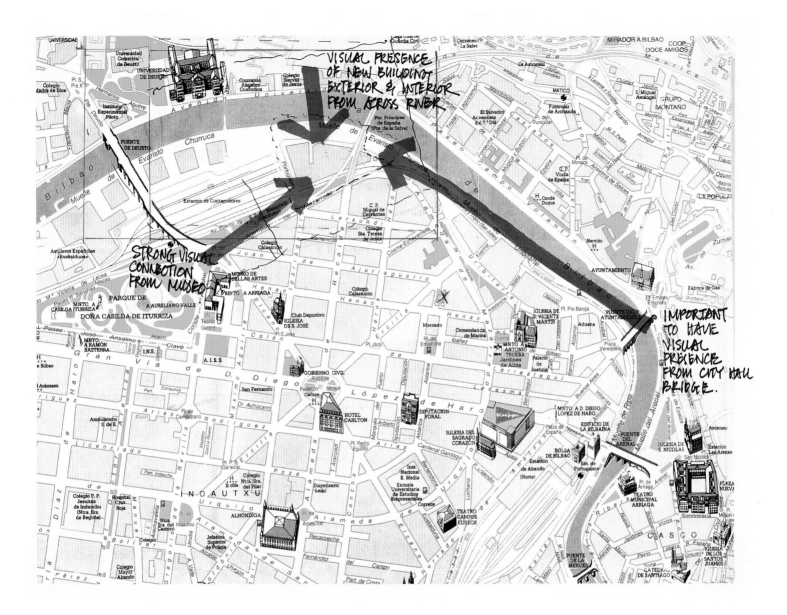

Map of Bilbao, with Gehry's handwritten notes, July 7, 1991.

The riverfront site the Guggenheim Museum Bilbao now occupies, as it appeared in December 1991.

While describing this run, Krens had a flashback to his very first visit, on April 9, when, at the end of the day, after flying over the city by helicopter to visit the Basque president, he was driven by car from the airport across the top of the ridge, where he took in a spectacular panoramic view of the stretch of land along the river, looking across to the Teatro Arriaga, the Museo de Bellas Artes, and the Universidad de Deusto. Adjacent to the river was a parcel of land with an abandoned brick lumber mill on it. In the middle of its decayed roof stood a single smokestack. Krens recollected, "None of the tracks had been removed from the factory complex, and around and underneath the bridge there were a lot of abandoned cars. It was clear that this part of the riverfront had not been particularly well used. I came back several times. And it may have been, now that I think about it, that I had basically invited Frank to confirm the argument against the Alhóndiga…with this thing already in mind, because the point was that the only way you could do a great building was to have a great site."

It was Juan Ignacio Vidarte, then the Director of Tax and Finance at the Regional Council of Bizkaia and the future Director General of the Guggenheim Museum Bilbao, who brought Gehry and Krens to the top of the hillside before dinner on May 20. In trying to remember the events of that day, Vidarte's first reaction was that it seemed to him that all visits had coalesced into one. Then, he distinctly recalled that he had focused on pointing out the Alhóndiga on the other side of the Nervión River. "The idea was to kill two birds with one stone," he said, to redevelop a dilapidated landmark as well as turn it into a museum for modern and contemporary art.[5] It came back to him that Gehry had asked about the bend in the river, and that he could not explain why such a central place was such a waste. Vidarte also mentioned that afterward, during dinner, when Krens agreed with Gehry's dismissal of the Alhóndiga site, there was great apprehension among the Basques. To them, the shift to the river seemed an impossible obstacle, because as far as they knew, the riverbank consisted of many sections of private property, some of it owned by institutions dependent on the central Spanish government. They therefore thought Krens was trying to block the project. Later, upon inquiry, it turned out to be a proposition that could be carried out after all.

In discussing whether Gehry's perspective on the events of May 20 might differ from Vidarte's and his own, Krens said, "Well, I believe in contradiction at certain parts of the design process; I'm not sure that I believe in different views in certain parts of the historical process. We saved every piece of paper on it.... It's not a question of my view or recollection versus Frank's view or recollection or Juan Ignacio's view or recollection, the point is that there was and is an accurate progression of information."

Nevertheless, there *are* three diverging narratives, though they conjure up one single vision post factum: the inevitability of the Bilbao Guggenheim's site on the Nervión River, roughly between the Puente de la Salve and the Puente de Deusto. In the words of Roland Barthes, "a text's unity lies not in its origin but in its destination."[6]

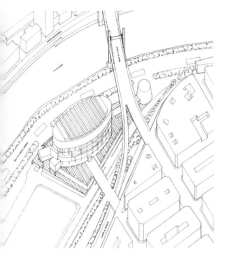

left and below: Arata Isozaki's entry to the Guggenheim Museum Bilbao design competition, July 1991.

On the Architect's Selection Process and Preliminary Program Statement

After the Basque Administration cleared the purchase of the new river location, the next step was to formulate a relationship between the site's main characteristics and the new museum. The Puente de la Salve, a large bridge to the east, had to be integrated into the site, as did the Muelle de Evaristo Churruca, a road along the riverfront to the north. On the south side, the scale and character of the buildings on the Alameda de Mazarredo, a large avenue, had to be taken into account for the new project to fit into the fabric of the city. Dr. Heinrich Klotz, formerly the Director of the Deutsches Architeckturmuseum in Frankfurt and a specialist in contemporary architecture, was asked to act as an advisor/referee in the architectural selection process. The Executive Committee of the Guggenheim Museum Bilbao Foundation, chaired by the Honorable Josu Bergara, was to choose the architect. A brief competition, involving an American, a European, and an Asian architect, all of whom Krens could recommend, was agreed upon. Isozaki, from Japan, was at that time already engaged as the architect of the Guggenheim Museum SoHo; occupying two floors of a block-long industrial building in downtown New York, it was scheduled to open in June 1992, concurrent with the newly restored Solomon R. Guggenheim Museum on Fifth Avenue and the opening of a tower addition, designed by Gwathmey Siegel and Associates Architects, to the Frank Lloyd Wright building. Gehry was selected as the American, and the European participant became the Viennese team of Wolf D. Prix and Helmut Swiczinsky, known as Coop Himmelblau, which had just won second place in the design competition for the ZKM/Center for Art and Media Technology in Karlsruhe, Germany, a proposal that had impressed Krens.

On June 26, Krens sent each architect the same memorandum about the selection procedure. They all made a site visit at the end of June or early July, and, without exception, started to sketch. The organizers set no restrictions on the terms of presentation: "Whatever they thought would communicate their concept for the building" would suffice. The selection committee was not interested in technicalities and details; they were after an impression of the

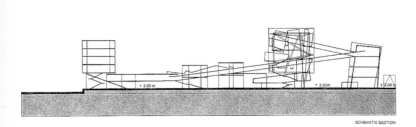

SCHEMATIC SECTION

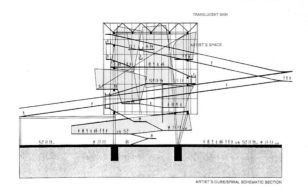

ARTIST'S CUBE/SPIRAL SCHEMATIC SECTION

Coop Himmelblau's entry to the
Guggenheim Museum Bilbao
design competition, July 1991.

overall vision of each architect. For instance, instead of figuring out a specific number of
galleries, the architects were to give rough estimates of scale and indicate general types of
exhibition spaces. Krens explained that the committee tried to avoid overdesign in the beginning in order not to have to battle about making changes later on. Only after the selection
was made would the explicit design process start, as if from scratch.

One remarkable feature of the future museum was the unusual ratio of 1:2 between gallery
spaces and all other museum facilities, feasible because of the special partnership with the
Solomon R. Guggenheim Foundation. Krens explained that it would not make sense to dupli-
cate services available in New York; as a result, less office space would be needed: "Our staff
in New York is 350 people. In Bilbao it would be only about 150 people, but Bilbao is twice
as large so there's a significant capital operating improvement due to running these two museums together." Bilbao could therefore be a museum favoring spaces for exhibiting the art.

By July 20, the architectural proposals had been submitted and delivered to the Frankfurterhof
Hotel in Frankfurt. Isozaki sent in sketches of a rather monolithic building, only faintly imply-
ing a connection to the Puente de la Salve, which was a requirement of the program. Coop
Himmelblau and Gehry both provided sketches as well as approximate models. Both planned
to build underneath the bridge while literally engaging both sides of it. Coop Himmelblau
preserved the old lumber mill with the smokestack as an integral element in their scheme;
Gehry did not. Both architects made accommodations for an extremely large gallery, another
programmatic prerequisite in order to house such complex pieces from the Guggenheim collection as Dan Flavin's light installations, or, as it later turned out, a 172-ton steel sculpture,
entitled *Snake*, by Richard Serra, consisting of three curves 4 meters high and 30 meters long,
built specifically for the space.

The aim of the selection committee was to choose a building that would be greater than the
sum of its parts and with a strong iconic identity of its own so that people would want to visit

the building for itself, while being respectful of the art to be shown in it: The inescapable analogy was Wright's Guggenheim Museum on Fifth Avenue. The neutral box concept was definitely rejected; instead, frequent references were made to Jørn Utzon's Sydney Opera House (1956–73) to clarify the case in point. "It was not immediate that it was going to be Frank," Krens stated. Coop Himmelblau "had done a very sensitive job.... The rectilinear shapes were actually going to be translated and suspended inside the grid.... You walked into spaces of different shapes, but because of the glow at night, the skin seemed to be eliminated. This was a very interesting idea." But in the end, it was Gehry's proposal for the Guggenheim Museum Bilbao that was selected during the course of meetings on July 20 and 21.

left: Guggenheim Museum
Bilbao, north elevation,
July 7, 1991.
Ink on López de Haro stationery,
21 x 29.8 cm.

below: Guggenheim Museum
Bilbao, north elevation,
July 7, 1991.
Ink on López de Haro stationery
(verso), 21 x 29.8 cm.

The Origins of the Bilbao Guggenheim

or the story of the architect's initial sketches, how they were programmatically translated, sculpturally defined, sometimes creatively misinterpreted, and shifted toward the building of a rough model, all within a span of less than two weeks

On July 5 and 6, 1991, Gehry, accompanied by his wife Berta, who speaks Spanish fluently, returned to Bilbao, this time no longer as an advisor but as a competitor reviewing the new site. On the morning of the 7th, having returned to the Hotel López de Haro after touring the site, about a five-minute walk away, he began to sketch his first impressions on the front and back of the hotel stationery; in these fast scrawls and mere annotations, the hand functions as an immediate tool of the mind. Moving the pen to occupy space on the paper, Gehry began to explore and familiarize himself with the site. He scaled up the components in relation to the existing buildings along the Alameda de Mazarredo. The natural slope running down to the riverfront suggested to Gehry, in search of a form, a cluster of buildings laid out along the lines of an amphitheater, which would give the museum a clear identification. He focused on an interaction, which had not existed before, between the vacant riverfront below and the urban area on the plateau above. According to the city's redevelopment plans, the area was to be transformed into a green valley, but Gehry did not want to lose the industrial feeling of the waterfront as it appeared at the base of the city.

The sketch on the back of the stationery shows the architect's vision of a tree-lined avenue connecting the site to the Museo de Bellas Artes. He thought of a spacious public area, a water garden, and a private counterpart — the museum — reachable by a ramp. Ramps also figure prominently in the sketch on the front of the page, which, next to a restaurant in sculptural form winding around the corner of the riverfront view and progressing onto the west elevation, shows to the east the Puente de la Salve, with two pylons sticking out into the water. The sloping space underneath the bridge, with its road deck stretching over it like a

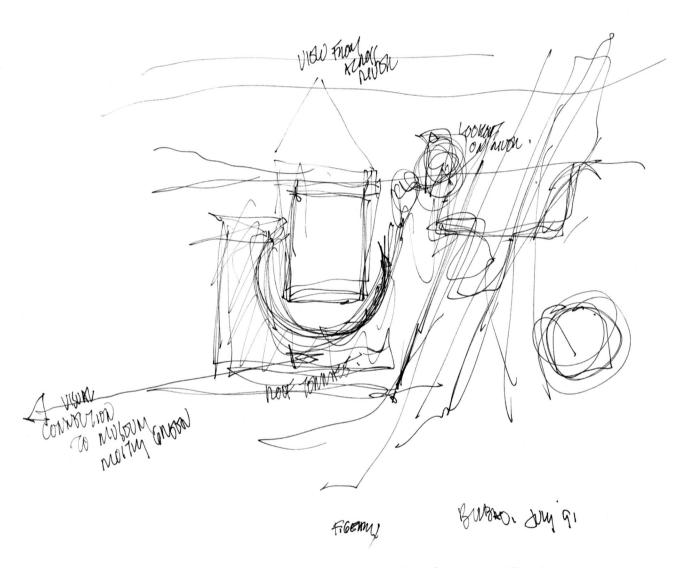

Guggenheim Museum Bilbao, plan, July 7, 1991. Ink on paper, 23 x 30.5 cm.

Temporary amphitheater for the 1984 World's Fair, New Orleans.

roof, suggests an outdoor amphitheater, while the protruding pylons might form a proscenium. A boat could come up the river and function as a stage. This concept, arising in immediate reaction to what he saw before him, has overtones of an earlier proposal by Gehry for a temporary, 5,000-seat covered amphitheater built for the World's Fair in New Orleans, Louisiana, in 1984. Strong analogies can be made: the New Orleans site was located on a wharf along the Mississippi River; the semicircular roof, tilted toward the river, was supported by columns behind the seating area and at the stage; a structural proscenium behind the stage area framed events along the river, much like Gehry intended for the pylons of the Puente de la Salve.

"I was not as conscious that it [the Bilbao Guggenheim] had something to do with what I did before until later," the architect stated, "because you know, I'm just looking at what I see. I tend to live in the present, and what I see is what I do. And what I do is I react. Then I realize that I did it before. I think it is like that because you can't escape your own language. How many things can you really invent in your lifetime? You bring to the table certain things. What's exciting, you tweak them based on the context and the people: Krens, Juan Ignacio, the Basques, their desire to use culture, to bring the city to the river. And the industrial feeling, which I'm afraid they are going to lose, for there's a tendency to make Washington Potomac Parkway out of the riverfront.... See, the bridge is like a gritty anchor. You take the bridge out and it's a whole different ballgame. So I think I was responding to the bridge, the toughness of the waterfront, its industrial character. The program Tom [Krens] came up with was MASS MoCA, big industrial volumes of space...and I knew all of that when I started sketching."

The more elaborate of the pair of schematic sketches, a chunky building with the explanatory note "roof terraces," echoes, in a way, the Alhóndiga; it opens up into a half-circular form around a rectangular water garden, which edges the river. The view is drawn from across the river; again, a strong visual connection with the Museo de Bellas Artes is called for and stressed in a jotting accompanied by a directional arrow. The words "mostly green" are a shorthand for the possibility of a park development between the old and the new museums. A "lookout on the river" and a high "reader" in the form of a tower, placed on the other side of the bridge to "capture" it, are drawn as two sculptural shapes, which, in their expanse of circular motion, become masses. Slight thickenings of line demarcate the beginning and ending of both outward and inward spiraling lines.

A simple sketch of a similar scheme locates a pivotal point, the entrance, at the crossing of the Alameda de Mazarredo and the Travesía de Portugalete. Ramps run down from the entry to the lookout, opposite from which the high reader is situated along the river, wedging into the Puente de la Salve. Gehry drew the river edge twice; in one case, he moved it up to make space for the water garden.

In all four early sketches, mapping out — the process of distributing basic features while getting to know the site — takes precedence over any other aesthetic design considerations. These sketches supplement a plan of the area, on which Gehry drew three red arrows, which bring the city into the site, and are annotated as follows: "visual presence of new building, exterior and interior from across the river," "strong visual connection from Museo," and "important to have visual presence from City Hall Bridge." Through the emphasis on the link between the city plateau and, below it, the incline toward the river (reutilized for cultural use), and in deciding which essential components of the museum were suited to the site in a scale relating to particular buildings in the surroundings, Gehry stimulated a dialogue between contextual structures and an innate formal vocabulary.

These first impressions and layout, although put on paper in haste, set a thinking pattern for the further development of the project; the spontaneity and eagerness of exploration of their inception, moreover, lend them an immediacy and vividness that, though they might be equalled in certain incisions done in the act of model making, cannot be maintained in a model as a whole. It is therefore all the more remarkable that Gehry's vision of, for instance, the riverfront elevation that appears in some of the sketches is preserved in the completed building itself. "I'm usually very happy when I'm drawing," Gehry said. "I do it when I'm either home alone, or on an airplane or when I am stuck in a hotel room and have to find something to amuse myself. Then, when I come back from a trip or whatever I do, I give the drawing to Edwin or to whoever is working on the model. It gives a starting point; usually with Edwin, he brings something to it."

Back in Los Angeles, during Gehry's absence, a schematic model was prepared roughly in accordance with the preliminary program sent by the Guggenheim staff at the end of June. At the request of the architect, it was to be brought by his project designer, Edwin Chan, to New York, Gehry's next stop after Bilbao. At that point the model consisted merely of a lightweight travel kit: some elemental ground-plan shapes made of basswood glued onto foamcore, representing three rectangular floors of 5,000 square meters, 6 meters high, or two larger ones of 12,000 square meters. A ziggurat and an octagon of tapering floors, which were arbitrarily

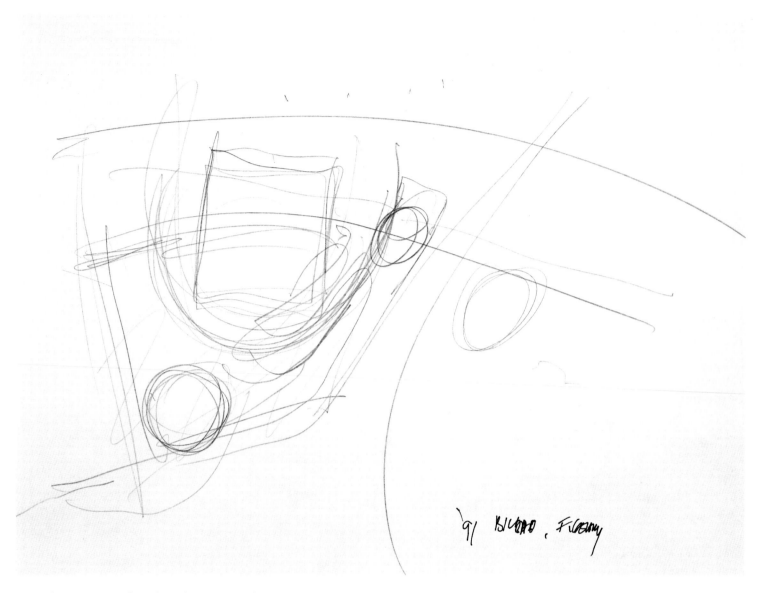

Guggenheim Museum Bilbao, plan, July 7, 1991. Pencil on paper, 23 x 30.5 cm.

chosen, served as alternative forms. Rounded, squared, and triangular recycled remnants of wood were to function as sculptural object shapes eventually to be transformed into galleries, a restaurant, or other museum facilities. Larger wood blocks of different heights represented the existing surrounding city fabric. They approximated in scale the apartment buildings on the quay across the river, while the number of floors was estimated from photographs taken on the site.

On July 9, Gehry and Chan met in the New York office of the architect Peter Eisenman and worked all morning in one of the conference rooms. While the first four sketches were done in response to the site, in the temporary model, which Gehry treated as an exercise to get into scale, he received some factual information about the requirements of the preliminary program, and about how much "stuff" was to go on the site, so that he could start "to carve it in my head." It simply gave him something to work against. For instance, in having discovered "nodal points" in the ground plan, such as the entrance or the restaurant, and in having arrived at an understanding of how they functioned through his earlier sketching, he was ready to represent them three-dimensionally in the model: "I put these little bumps in it, for I know I'm gonna do stuff; o.k., surround the box."

Gehry was resolved to make the south elevation toward the Alameda de Mazarredo rectilinear in relation to the existing office and apartment buildings, which date from the late nineteenth and early twentieth centuries. The north view could then have more loose nautical imagery, sails or curved boat forms going with the flux of the river. Represented by a pile of blocks, the high reader on the other side of the bridge could house galleries devoted to individual artists. Gehry worked with Chan on an improvisatory roof form by covering the central part of the model with three wavy, sail-like scraps of white paper. As this gesture happened at the end of the morning, they left it at that. The next day, Chan flew back to Los Angeles to work out the changes in the model, while Gehry went on to Boston to work on his project for a Children's Museum, after which he was to return to Los Angeles on July 11.

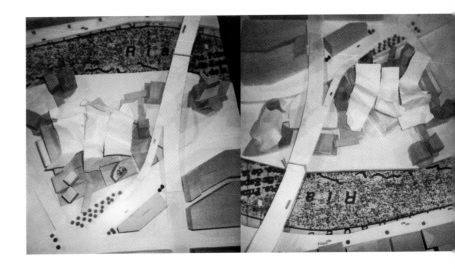

Schematic model as it appeared after the meeting between Chan and Gehry in New York on July 9, 1991.

The first of the next series of sketches, done on the airplane, carries the project a stage further. Two rectangular building components, consisting of several tapering floors, envelop a courtyard-like space on the south and west sides. On top of the structures several one-line circular contours indicate a future sculptural elaboration of some kind. A stretched-out squiggle represents a ramp along the west side. To the east, a strong physical connection links the main complex with the bridge through an amphitheater situated underneath it. The absence of the water garden does not necessarily mean that the idea is discarded; it may be stored temporarily, to be brought back when needed. The view is taken again from the river. The restaurant shape has gained plasticity through the emphatic spiraling of Gehry's fineliner pen, which leaves inscribed traces. A fervent ice hockey player, he likens drawing to skating across paper and loves the feeling of the felt pen sliding over it: "Everything connected with everything else seems freer, not taking your hands off. I love the free-flow."

The next sketch translates the ground plan into the first idea of what the riverfront elevation might look like. The physiognomy of the building, while still quite disembodied, begins to take on some features: the restaurant with spiraling ramp; the beginning of what Gehry singles out as the Great Hall, covered by sail-like shapes similar to the scraps of white paper in the model; and vertically fenestrated glass in front of its entrance. Three wavy lines, rhythmically running upward so that a layered look and depth formation is created, represent stepped up "volumes" behind the glass. "It's just the way I draw when I'm thinking," Gehry exclaimed in looking at the drawing not so long ago. "I think that way. I'm just moving the pen. I'm thinking about what I'm doing, but I'm sort of not thinking about my hands." A parallel can be drawn with automatic writing in the way Barthes defined it, "by entrusting the hand with the task of writing as quickly as possible what the head itself is unaware of."[7]

The architect often refers to his drawing as "scratching": "I'm looking through the paper to try to pull out the formal idea; it's like somebody drowning in the paper. And that's why I never think of them as drawing; I can't. Only after the fact when I look at them." In so doing,

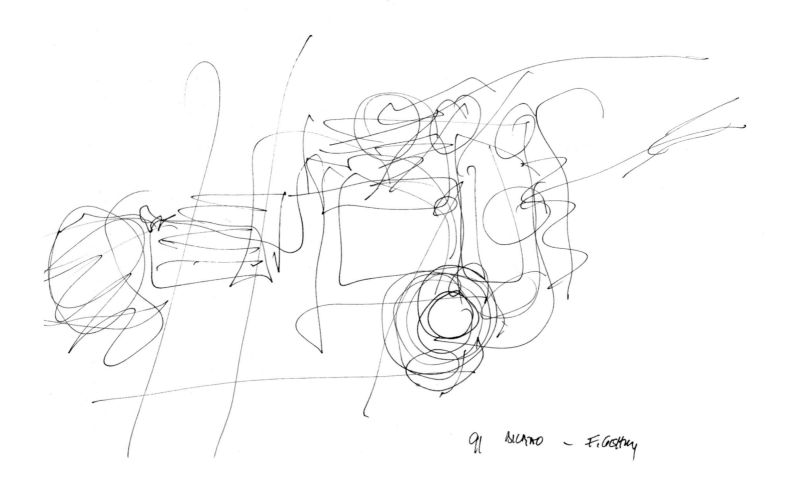

91 BILBAO - F. Gehry

facing page: Guggenheim Museum Bilbao, plan, July 11, 1991.
Ink on paper, 23 x 30.5 cm.

below: Guggenheim Museum Bilbao, north elevation, July 11, 1991.
Ink on paper, 23 x 30.5 cm.

Gehry shifts from being the author engaged in his semiautomatic scrawling/writing to assuming the role of the investigative reader ready to disentangle potential forms enmeshed within the multiple lines and contours caught in his drawings. Barthes argued that "a text is made of multiple writings, drawn from many cultures and entering into mutual relations of dialogue, parody, contestation, but there is one place where this multiplicity is focused and that place is the reader, not, as was hitherto said, the author."[8] Intuitively, Gehry succeeds in combining the conscious with the unconscious, schematic planning based on the preliminary program and circumstance of the site with semi-automatic scrawling/writing. Even after he puts down his felt pen, marking the end of the drawing stage, the creative process continues when the architect returns to his sketches as reader. Subsequently, he may discover accidental forms that may be added to his vocabulary or discarded later, all in the pursuit of but one goal: "Drawing is a tool. So is the model. Everything is a tool. The building is the only thing that means anything — the finished building."

In the third sketch, as Gehry recalled it, he was looking for chance images to occur, while at the same time consciously trying to integrate the bridge within the composition of the building: "I thought that if I had more site on the other side of the bridge, I would capture it more." Looking at the sketch recently, Gehry remarked on a prominent shape, curved like a ship's bow, on the east side of the bridge: "I don't know what happened to it. I lost it in the end. But, you know, I'm balancing the drawing; it became a composition too." As it turned out, that bow shape, an element tough and unusual enough to complement the "aesthetic irritant" of the bridge, popped up in the building process much later on as one of the sculptural side galleries near the entrance. Gehry continued: "And as I refine, I would start to say, well, this may have an atrium quality and these shapes might break into the scale of the city, and that might have a sculptural emphasis at the river. And at the same time, I'm also dealing with what the drawing looks like, while not losing the train of thought. I'm always fascinated that I can draw these lines unintentionally — like that little piece is beautiful. And these lines came out like a hammerhead snake. Sometimes I think snakes and fishes are all there are in the world."

The concept of a snake form first occurred in Gehry's work in 1981, in a project for a nursery school and children's museum to be located in downtown Los Angeles. Gehry and the sculptor Richard Serra were invited separately to design an object for it, but decided to work jointly. Serra was thinking about a coiling snake in tile next to a fish shape Gehry wanted to explore. The fish shape had come up earlier that year in a bridge design they had proposed for an exhibition at the Architectural League in New York entitled *Collaboration: Artists and Architects.* Two pylons, one designed by Gehry in the form of a gigantic fish emerging from the Hudson River, and the other by Serra in the form of an enormous tilted steel slab, were to anchor two sets of holding cables piercing the World Trade Center on the fish side, and the Chrysler Building on the canted side.

For an exhibition called *Follies: Architecture for the Late Twentieth-Century Landscape,* presented in 1983 at the Leo Castelli Gallery in New York, Gehry made a proposal for a prison on a pri-

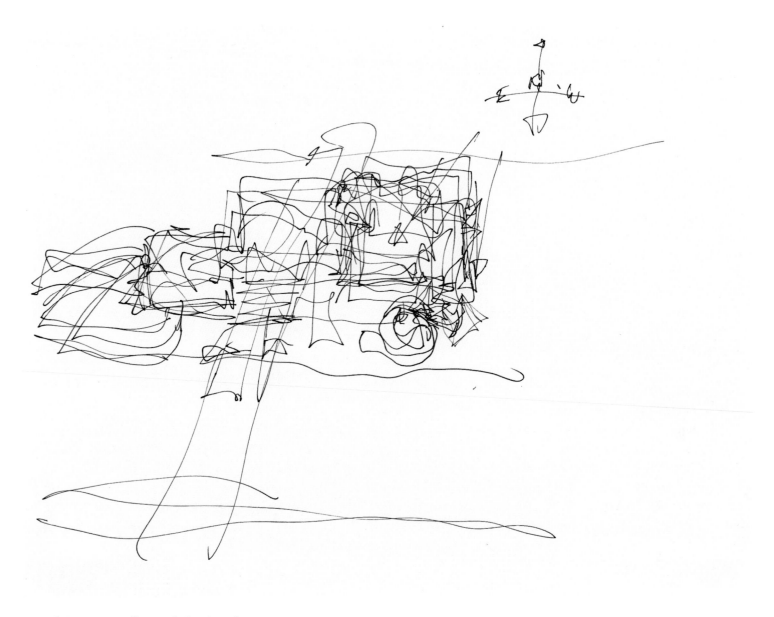

Guggenheim Museum Bilbao, north elevation, July 11, 1991.
Ink on paper, 23 x 30.5 cm.

Detail on facing page.

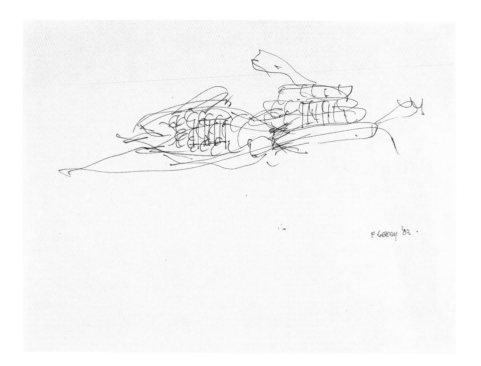

left and above: Folly designs for *Follies: Architecture for the Late Twentieth-Century Landscape* at Leo Castelli Gallery, New York, 1983.

vate estate in which he put the snake and the fish together. In describing the project, he stated, "I think that the primitive beginnings of architecture come from zoomorphic yearnings and skeletal images." Next to a glass pavilion in the form of the fish was a coiling snake, which was to be constructed of brick in order to give the building "the physical solidity associated with the word 'prison.'" Gehry deemed the snake a fitting emblem for the folly, as it evokes fear, and felt, moreover, that "the use of animate forms allows for a great deal of flexibility in adjusting the scale of the folly to the specific location and budget."[9]

During the process of executing a small model of the bridge project with Serra, Gehry realized that by making the fish scales out of overlapping glass tiles, rounded along one edge, he had inadvertently hit on a method of shingling adaptable to structures of any size. He began to apply this technique on a modest scale, using flints of Colorcore Formica to make lamps in the shape of fish and, occasionally, snakes. In 1986, for his 6.7 meter high *Standing Glass Fish* for the Walker Art Center, Gehry devised a large timber-and-steel armature to support diamond-shaped scales of .6 centimeter tempered glass. In the following year, his Fishdance restaurant was completed along the waterfront in Kobe, Japan. It contained a copper-clad spiraling angular snake form and a 21.3 meter high fish sculpture made of chainlink mesh.

Two years before the Bilbao project, Gehry proposed a snake pavilion — 9.7 meters in diameter at its base and about 9.12 meters high — to be constructed of a gold-colored stainless-steel frame with copper cladding, for Library Square in Los Angeles. This proposal was rejected, but in 1991–92, as he was designing the Bilbao Guggenheim, he built a 54 meter long and

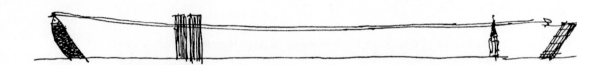

Frank Gehry and Richard Serra, bridge design for *Collaboration: Artists and Architects*
at the Architectural League of New York, 1981. Ink on paper, 20.6 x 27.3 cm.

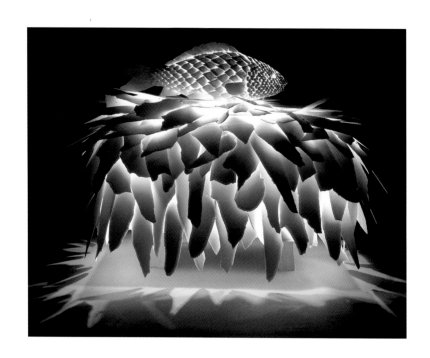

above: Fish lamp designed by Gehry and made of Colorcore Formica, 1984.

facing page: Standing Glass Fish, 1986.
Wire, wood, glass, steel, silicone, Plexiglas, and rubber, 6.71 x 4.27 x 2.59 m.
Walker Art Center, Minneapolis, Gift of Anne Pierce Rogers in honor of her grandchildren Anne and Will Rogers, 1986.

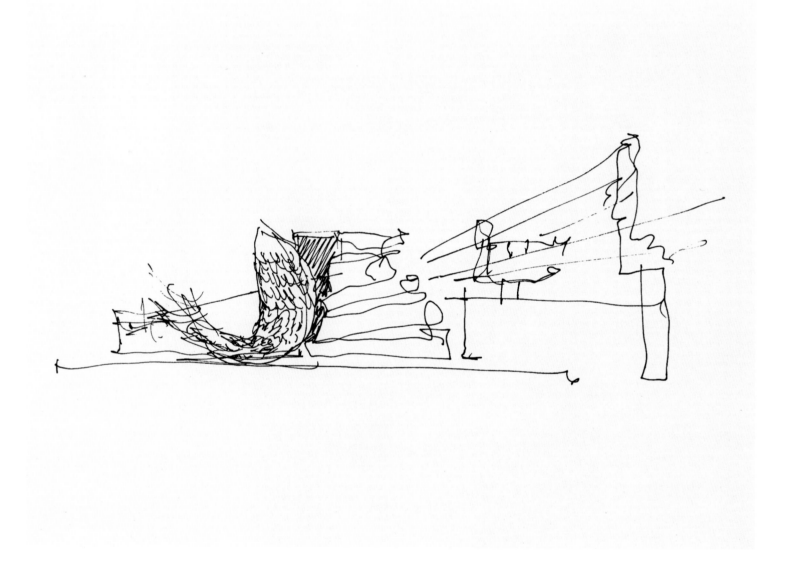

above: Fishdance restaurant, Kobe, Japan, east elevation, 1986.
Ink on paper, 23 x 30.5 cm.

facing page: Fishdance restaurant, Kobe, Japan (1987).

Fish sculpture, Villa Olímpica complex, Barcelona (1992).

35 meter tall, highly abstracted, floating-fish sculpture, which functioned as a shading device for a retail court along a waterfront promenade at the Villa Olímpica complex in Barcelona. Indeed, snakes and fishes continue to be on the architect's mind; he attributes his fascination with the fish form to a vivid childhood recollection involving his grandmother, with whom he went to the market on Thursdays: "We'd go to the Jewish market, we'd buy a live carp, we'd take it home to her house in Toronto, we'd put it in the bathtub and I would play with this goddamn fish for a day until the next day she'd kill it and make gefilte fish." [10]

right: The factory that originally occupied the site of the Guggenheim Museum Bilbao.

below: Guggenheim Museum Bilbao, north elevation, July 1991.
Ink on paper, 23 x 30.5 cm.

Looking for materials at hand on the site along the Nervión River, Gehry drew the west elevation of the Bilbao project with three brick smokestacks in a row on top of the long rectangular
building, while a ramp, an image not unlike an oceanliner, came down on the side. In front of
the Great Hall arose a restaurant in an abstracted snake shape. The striations of both building components were thought of as representing brick, a distant echo of the original brick
factory with the smokestack in the center that once occupied the site. The material of brick
and the desirability of a smaller, easily adaptable structure — the restaurant — in front of the
larger building probably gave Gehry the association with the snake folly. Yet the snake as symbol was at odds with a museum concept, for in his mind it stands for hostility.

Under the time constraint of two weeks, Gehry naturally returned to the forms with which he was most familiar. Manipulating the snake in this new context required ridding it of its past associations, sloughing off the old skin in order to give way to a new "little piece" — which Gehry identified as "bootlike" — discovered next to the hammerhead snake in the earlier sketch. Over time, a more refined and solidified version of this form became a two-level gallery. In the next sketch, two rectangular larger buildings appear, as do the Great Hall, with sail-like covering, the boot-shaped gallery, and the snake-form restaurant, now transformed into a single coiling ramp. The floor plan is shown twice in an effort to make a balanced composition on the page. In the upper plan, in front of the boot shape Gehry liked so much, little dots indicate a reflecting pool. In the lower section, a grouping of regular, squarish galleries is substituted for the ship's bow on the east side of the bridge.

Guggenheim Museum Bilbao,
plans, July 1991.
Ink on paper, 23 x 30.5 cm.

'91 BILBAO . F.GEHRY

Guggenheim Museum Bilbao, north elevation (left), atrium (top right), and skylights (bottom right), July 1991. Ink on paper, 23 x 30.5 cm.

In scribing once more the schematic plan and simultaneously evoking what the exterior of the building might look like, the architect's imagination oscillated between sense perception and functional demands. One sheet shows, on the right side, a rather general design for the atrium, and, underneath, a row of skylights. In the scheme, the sail-like covering of the Great Hall occupying the center rises higher than the bridge, and figures as a pronounced sculptural form on top of a cluster of buildings. A nearly frantic intertwining of lines back and forth breaks the scale down into several smaller elements next to the spiraling snakelike shape, which sits on a pedestal, and might protrude into the water. Thin long shapes show an attempt to put a ramp or flight of stairs into the courtyard. The same repertory of elements, including two ziggurat-shaped, large warehouse-type buildings enclosing the west and south sides, are complemented for the first time by a long gallery running underneath the bridge.

Detail of drawing on previous page.

Frederick R. Weisman Museum, Minneapolis (1990).

The two images on the side are each of a double nature. Both take stock provisionally of how the atrium is to function and constitute tryouts for a formal vocabulary. To start with, the row of skylights at the lower end of the sheet is an image produced by suggestion, and therefore open to many analogies; seen in context, however, it has specific connotations. Reminiscent of the seashell shapes that distinguish the Sydney Opera House — often mentioned by Krens as the kind of landmark the committee was looking for — the row of skylights also bears a relation to the large billowing, sail-like screens made from stainless-steel panels that catch and bounce the southern light back onto the north wall of the Frederick R. Weisman Art Museum in Minneapolis, Minnesota, a project Gehry was working on at the time. These monumental fish-sail shapes, pushed beyond pure sculpture into function, would give the Bilbao building an iconic quality. Renzo Piano's more machinelike light scoops for the Menil Collection in Houston, Texas, also come to mind. But above all, the fluid motion of the skylight forms corresponds to the imagery of fish.

Like the experimental snake, which appeared and then exited, the fish serves as a temporary iconic form to identify the building, but the meaning of the fish imagery is more complex. In 1985, Gehry stated: "I kept drawing it and sketching it and it started to become for me like a symbol for a certain kind of perfection that I couldn't achieve with my buildings. Eventually whenever I'd draw something and I couldn't finish the design, I'd draw the fish as a notation ... that I want this to be better than just a dumb building. I want it to be more beautiful."[11] At this time, Gehry had arrived at a stage in which he was no longer so much interested in the fish as an object. The seductive quality of the iridescent, overlapping shards in Formica or glass led him to rethink the fish as skin, thus dissociating it from its predominant image. Subsequently, Gehry derived an abstract shape from the fish image by cutting off its head and tail; the resulting shape was utilized for a lead enclosure to exhibit small objects in a retrospective of his work at the Walker Art Center in 1986. About two years later, a 16.4 meter long "fish" form was constructed with wooden ribs sheathed in a galvanized sheet-metal skin to house a conference room for the Chiat/Day temporary offices in Venice, California.

Abstracted fish studies continue to intrigue Gehry. "The fish shape got me into moving freely," he said in July 1990. "I learned how to make a building that was much more plastic, and the first chance at that was the Furniture Museum at Vitra.... I started to use those shapes, but now I think the thing is to cut it back and see how little of that you can do and still get that sense of immediacy and movement." The fish image, its form and appearance refined in drawing after drawing, changes from an object with iconic identity to an innovative material application of a frame bearing a shimmering skin. And in exploring the theme intuitively he learned how to make double curves in buildings. In the Bilbao Guggenheim, "fish" — truncated, without head or tail, transformed into leaf or boatlike shapes and applied in some of the side galleries — is endowed with a more elusive metaphorical quality, and comes to signify fluid, continuous motion; it is a tangible sculptural abstraction vivifying the building.

above and facing page: Vitra International Furniture Museum,
Weil am Rhein, Germany (1989).

The image above the skylights-as-sails shows a pedestal that functions as a container for technical facilities, complemented by three freely designed, overlapping plastic forms sitting on it, which in turn are topped by two functional skylights, the whole conjuring up bottle shapes. Earlier, Gehry had deduced that the complexity of the American Center in Paris, the design of which he began in 1988 and the construction of which was under way during the competition phase of the Bilbao Guggenheim, derives essentially from two masses in tension: "I was thinking of buildings in terms of bottles. You put them together and there's an energy that you don't get from a bottle alone. They have an effect on each other."[12] The configuration of bottle and jar shapes originates with the Winton Guest House, a project from 1983–87; in its small scale and use of Platonic geometrical shapes, placed closely together in the landscape of Wayzata, Minnesota, it embodies a highly sculptural concept. Gehry considers it his most refined work, and refers to it as "a tight complex, like a still life, like a Morandi." At the time, he felt that "the breakthrough for me in this house was the idea of cracks between the buildings, wedge-shaped cracks that serve to differentiate the parts of the pure forms and suggest that they are complete forms because of this cleavage."[13] And, in fact, the approach of interstices in between sculptural shapes returns in an altered state in the Guggenheim atrium.

below left: Winton Guest House, Wayzata, Minnesota (1987).

below right: American Center, Paris (1994).

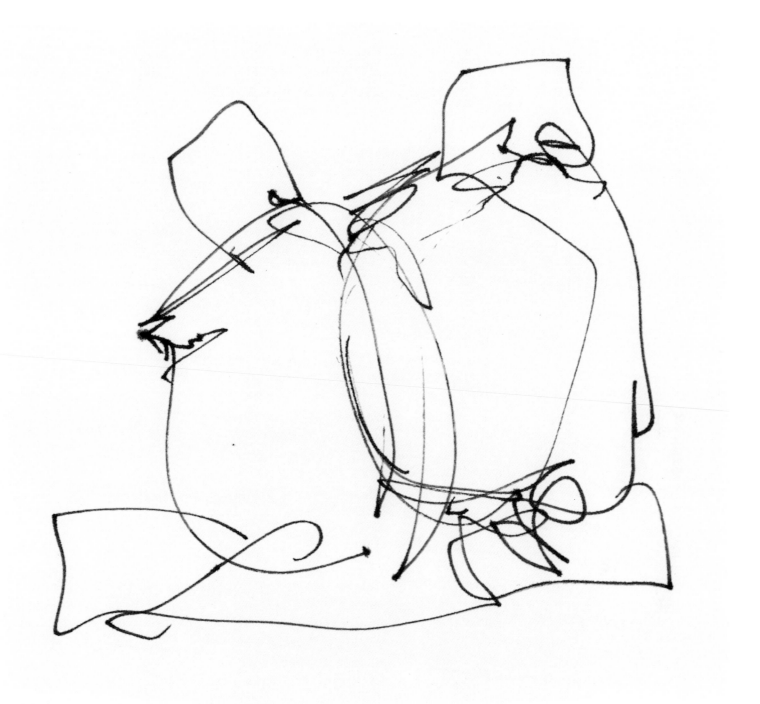

Detail of page 53.

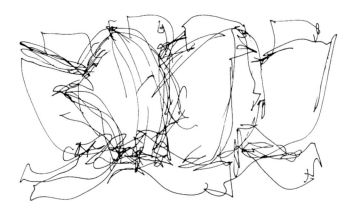

The three bottle shapes in the drawing, when considered in relation to the row of skylights, may take on the equivalent form of such freely flowing sail-like volumes as well. They closely resemble similar volumes set on a wavy pedestal in the Walt Disney Concert Hall, the design of which Gehry was then finishing. Inspired by the billowing fir-ply ceiling of the hall's interior, which creates the effect of a ship's hull, Gehry had taken the curvilinear vocabulary outside, and had wrapped the exterior with large gestural sail-like volumes. Coincidentally, in spring 1991, he had come upon an exhibition, entitled *Mirror of Empire: Dutch Marine Art of the Seventeenth Century*, at the Toledo Museum of Art in Ohio. Gehry had seen examples of this genre of painting before, but only then did it occur to him that there was a correlation between them and what he was trying to achieve in his architecture: "I came at it differently, because I sail a boat. I was just trying to get a sense of movement in my buildings, a subtle kind of energy. And making a building that has a sense of movement appeals to me, because it knits into the larger fabric of movement of the city.... Buildings are part of living in the city and it changes; there's a transient quality."

Walt Disney Concert Hall,
east elevation, May 1991.
Ink on paper, 23 x 30.5 cm.

Walt Disney Concert Hall,
east elevation (top), section
(center, left), east elevation
(center, right), and detail of
east elevation (bottom).
Ink on paper, 23 x 30.5 cm.

facing page: Frederick R. Weisman Art Museum, Minneapolis (1990).

above: Frederick R. Weisman Art Museum, Minneapolis, west elevation, October 1990. Ink on paper, 23 x 30.5 cm.

The fleeting trapped within the immutable creates a sense of displacement so necessary for an architecture embodying sculptural or pictorial, emotive relationships. Gehry's Frederick R. Weisman Art Museum (1990–93) encompasses this quality. To the west, overlooking the Mississippi River and the urban skyline of Minneapolis beyond, the architect had envisioned the façade folding in and out like a pleated skirt, so that the windows would look up and down the river. In search of a principle that could bring about a rationale of fragmentation in a smaller scale while at the same time holding the scattering components together, he had hit upon an image attributable to his experience in steering the bow of a sailboat nearer the wind: "There's a point in sailing called the turning point," Gehry said, "when the boat is coming about and you are turning into the wind; for a split second as you flatten the boat, and the wind is out of the sails, just before the flutter — the sail's luff it's called — that leading edge gets this movement, it's quite beautiful, in the space of the two sails. I began to use it in Minnesota in the façade."

This freezing of a specific moment in time reflects a yearning for immediacy that he had "absorbed in his psyche" upon experiencing the bronze statue of the Charioteer (ca. 470 B.C.), made by an unknown sculptor for the Sanctuary of Apollo in Delphi, Greece: "It has as much to do with the sense of putting life in it; even though it's a static figure, it has that incredible immediacy. [The sculptor] probably succeeded because that tradition of casting in bronze had been handed down from generation to generation." In an August 1991 sketch for the Bilbao project, made after the completion of the competition model, the ground plan is reiterated and three image-notations are drawn on the side, one of which is treated like the Weisman Museum façade; once again, Gehry had in mind an instant of released plastic freedom and beauty, the result not of a contrived feat of the extraordinary, but rather of the transformation of the accessible ordinary.

The sketch shows a ground plan in which the long gallery running underneath the bridge serves as a step-up not only for a gallery on top of the bridge but also as a support for the tower on its east end; thus, the long gallery also functions as a pedestal. The tower and the gallery, in addition to a sculptural skylight on top of the gallery, are treated as separate object/sculptures united by the same base. The loose, bigger gestural image at the top of the sheet resembles the Walt Disney Concert Hall (as seen in a March 1990 elevation); the notations underneath exemplify a tightly fragmented stainless-steel corrugation, like the façade and north elevation of the Weisman Museum. All three image-notations are, to Gehry, reminders of ways to deform the conventional curtain-wall construction, pushing it out of restrictive architectural limits into a more sculptural, curvilinear approach in metal.

Walt Disney Concert Hall, east elevation (detail), March 1990. Ink on paper, 23 x 30.5 cm.

Guggenheim Museum Bilbao, plan (left, top), north elevation (left, bottom),
and annotations, August 1991. Ink on paper, 23 x 30.5 cm.

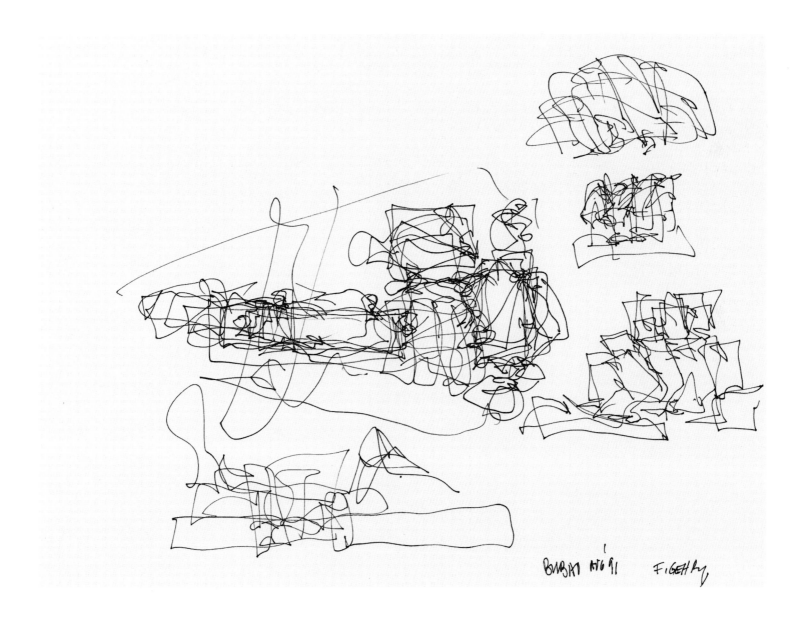

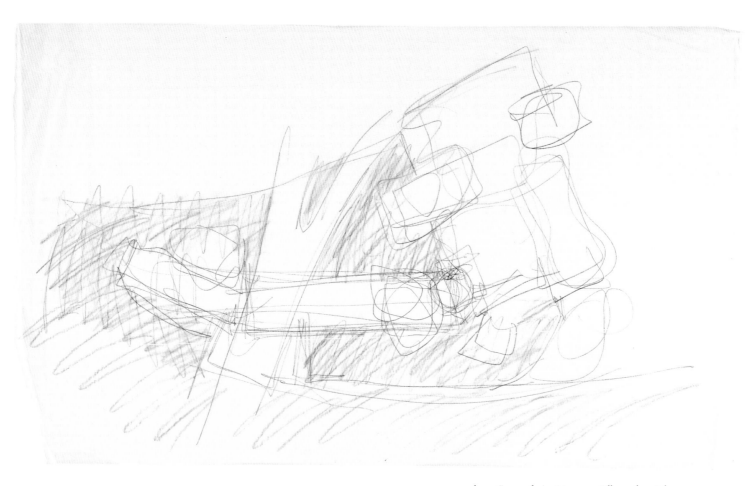

above: Guggenheim Museum Bilbao, plan, July 1991.
Colored pencil and pencil on tracing paper, 50 x 82.6 cm.

facing page: Guggenheim Museum Bilbao, plan, July 1991.
Colored pencil and pencil on tracing paper, 50 x 82.6 cm.

Two "conceptual plans" elaborate on the series of sketches drawn during the flight back from Boston to Los Angeles. One sketch, to be annotated later with specifics for inclusion in the competition book accompanying the model, addresses the planning of larger exhibition spaces combined with several smaller galleries, each sizable enough to house a group of works or a site-specific installation by a single artist. Two water gardens, intended not only as gentle barriers but also, in their reflection of the building, as enhancements of the sculptural effect, run along the waterfront elevation and in front of the long gallery on the east elevation. While the amphitheater is still in place underneath the bridge and about to be carried into the model stage, the restaurant as ramp has traded places with one of the galleries; it now has moved to the end of the long gallery.

Guggenheim Museum Bilbao, plan, July 1991.
Ink on paper, 23 x 30.5 cm.

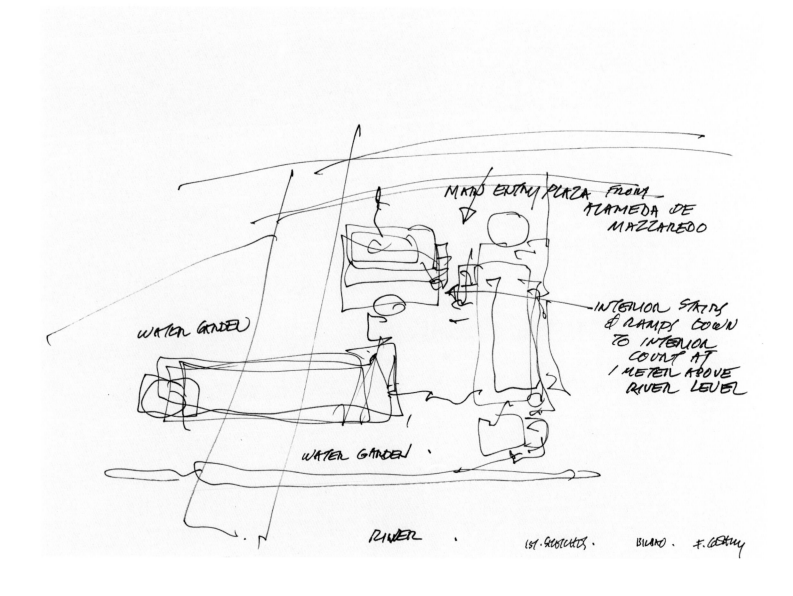

Once more, in a simplified sketch, Gehry summarizes the basics of his scheme: two warehouse-type building elements, surrounding a plazalike Great Hall and creating some definition of an enclosure, with a huge hangar-shaped gallery abutting the hall and continuing underneath the bridge to the east. Each of the three large components, in the scale of the bridge, is supplemented with at least one or more smaller sculptural forms to achieve a more human scale and texture as part of the riverfront and as an entry punctuation. A ziggurat geometry with sculptural edges characterizes the appearance. Gehry refers to the concept of a large, simple building functioning as a backdrop against which a smaller sculptural building is situated as "a Madonna and Child" scale relationship; he recalls encountering this effect in Japan, where high-rises accidentally coexist with much smaller temples.

"I was just trying to understand the scale of it, in relation to the site. And see what kind of footprint I was going to have," Gehry said in 1996, upon looking again at these sketches, "and to see what areas these galleries were. I knew he [Krens] wanted a big long one, because he talked about it, and he talked about MASS MoCA. I knew we wanted blocks. The ziggurat was a residual amphitheater, where you stepped down. I had just visited a quarry, and gotten excited about making some very blocky thing, and then about creating a public space with a cover on it, but not closed." In the same sketch, the main entry plaza from the Alameda de Mazarredo has been widened, resulting in more space between entry and offices. Interior staircases and ramps lead down into the Great Hall's court, raised 1 meter above the average river level as a precaution against flooding; later, the rise was increased by an additional 2 meters in order to comply with local regulations.

Gehry's approach in the series of sketches done on the plane ranges from wielding the pen with total control to nearly letting the lines flow by themselves, fluid, mobile, punctuated by little jolts, starts, and stops. He has not only begun to take hold of the complexities of the site but at the same time allowed for mnemonic images to surface. Allowing the pen to take possession of the space expedites the absorption into the imagination of problems due to the program requirements, leading to their clarification. Elements shift and are regrouped to contribute to a different kind of understanding, a leap from the conditional, technical aspects of building into unrestrained, intuitive sense perception, into sculptural architecture. From here on, a delicate process of cutting apart while holding together takes place, a going back and forth from sketches into models in order to solve problems and refine the plastic shapes of the building.

The individualistic activity of envisioning and problem solving through sketching assures Gehry privacy in the midst of life in the architectural office, where he is continuously interrupted by phone calls, client meetings, and other impositions on his time. From the solving of problems in the privacy of his drawing phase Gehry derives enough security to free-associate with his team, improvising unceasingly. There is a performance element in all of this, with clients, critics, artists, and friends passing by to give their input. From time to time, misinterpretations produced by the design team in the translation of Gehry's directions and annotated sketches into architectural elements even trigger new departures. Challenging incongruities may be accepted or rejected by the architect; in any case, such a working method lets chance play a role, preventing repetition and fixation on conventions.

Utilizing fugitive materials gathered on the premises, sometimes by others, combined with a reductive form of programming that minimizes overwhelming details, keeps the flow of the imagination going and induces Gehry to constantly see things anew. Once he has acquired a certain distance in time and place from the site, the architect sets himself up so that associative imagery can surface. Gehry traces this method to his youth; when he was about ten years old, he and his grandmother built cities on the floor from stuff found lying around the house: "I'm still doing the same thing with little boxes and trash and leftover pieces of wood. But the point is that if there is any thread of continuity in my view of 'the city' it stems from the fact that I've always thought of the city in sculptural terms and been interested in how the forms of a city create patterns of living.... The city is itself a sculpture that can be composed and in which relationships can be established." [14]

Having recaptured elemental truths discovered first in childhood through the act of stacking blocks, then through his "obsession" with fish, Gehry has next to transform them into structural correspondences of a certain measure and proportion. Along with the development of a formal vocabulary to suit technicalities of the specific program comes an emotive quality going beyond mere child's play. It is a state of being such as Charles Baudelaire wrote about in his essay "The Painter of Modern Life": "Genius is nothing more nor less than *childhood recovered* at will — a childhood now equipped for self-expression with manhood's capacities and a power of analysis which enables it to order the mass of raw material which it has involuntarily accumulated." [15]

The turning point in Gehry's thinking about the city was his 1976 design for the Jung Institute in Los Angeles, which went only as far as a single drawing. Within a compound surrounded by screen walls, which not only shut out the industrial debris littering the area but also

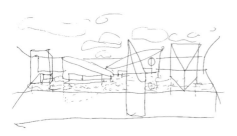

Jung Institute, conceptual sketch, 1976.
Ink on paper, 20.6 x 27.3 cm.

created "an intimacy with the sky," he placed several distinct object/structures, connecting them by water, in the form of a shallow pool, and by the sky: "The individual elements became pieces that you would discover by walking around them and seeing them play against each other sculpturally. This very simple manipulation of a very clear and minimal set of forms — a box, a wedge, an oval — produced a very interesting and complex interplay and set of interrelationships."[16]

In spite of being "anti-urban" in its separation from the neighborhood, Gehry sensed that the Jung Institute design, with its composition of overlapping, discrete pieces, could give rise to a certain kind of urbanism, and that in breaking down the scale of the elements that form a building, different, more human-scale connections would emerge. "I never started with the intention to develop architectural metaphors for urban experiences," he has said, "and I've never had the chance to do many urban complexes, but I have always explored forms and how they connect."[17]

In his approach to urbanism, Gehry has never directed himself toward the grandiosity of a Versailles; the opportunities he has had in urban planning have been more about the small gesture, but with catalytic impact. The architect Robert A. M. Stern wrote, "In all his work Gehry makes the grand gesture and then pulls it apart. He has the great gift to challenge us but not threaten us, to give us order and disorder without tyranny."[18] This effect is exemplified by three of Gehry's projects: the Loyola Law School (1981–84), comprising a block in the middle of a rough neighborhood in downtown Los Angeles; the Hollywood Library (1983–86), sited in a lot in the midst of urban chaos; and the Yale Psychiatric Institute (1985–86), occupying a block in the middle of a poor neighborhood in New Haven, Connecticut. "There's always just a small piece. And I guess, I've grown up that way, to accept that idea." Within that context, Gehry has shown an immensely subtle and even laid-back attitude toward the integration of his architecture into the surrounding neighborhood.

To take the Loyola Law School as a case in point, in accordance with the request of the clients, there was a need "in this funny wasteland" to create a place "that didn't upstage the neighbors," as Gehry expressed it. In working with that concept, the Loyola campus seen from the street is quite unassuming. Laid out along a simple site plan, a rather long three-story building housing faculty offices and spaces for student functions is combined in an L-shaped block with two smaller one-room buildings, a chapel, and a lecture hall. The three new structures are placed with their backs toward the street and are recessed so as not to dominate the adjacent neighborhood buildings. By association with the more complicated existing law-school building, "this simple building next to it enriched the old building and made the street more habitable." For security reasons, the school had him put a fence around the site: "I had to walk a tightrope between visual accessibility and the relationship to the street. Still, it isn't a solid wall; people can look in and even walk in but they really aren't supposed to." [19]

In contrast, within the campus, simplicity gives way to a wealth of texture, from yellow stucco and Finnish plywood to concrete and galvanized metal, which together with randomly positioned patches of landscaping and the baroque stairways on the outer side of the long build-

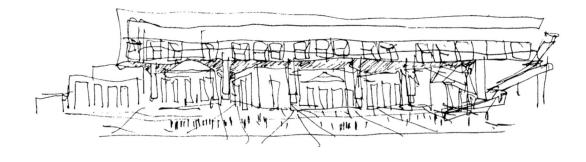

Loyola Law School, conceptual sketch, 1981.
Ink on paper, 23 x 30.5 cm.

ing create a dense overlay. Again, taking the neighborhood into account, the main wall of the long building is painted a bright color, hardly visible on the exterior, but on the court side functions like a stage set against which more characteristic, single buildings, in a small, human scale, are silhouetted in order to create a campus feeling. "I think the city is a fact you can't change," Gehry said in 1991. "How to include rather than exclude existing buildings was interesting to me, and also to put dissimilar objects next to one another; a lot of architecture builds itself with an implied wall."

Comparing his urbanistic approach to that of Le Corbusier, Gehry has paradoxically stated: "I'm more psychologically aware. Le Corbusier's approach was to say, 'I don't like you and I'm going to demolish you and throw you down to the ground and build something new and this is what I'm going to build.' I don't say that. I may not like you, but I don't tell I don't like you. I just come along, make my little mudpie and take over." Though this statement has a slightly Napoleonic ring to it, in practice it turns out that the architect has in mind a certain type of integration with the urban surroundings. How the concept of takeover works is clarified in another statement: "If you understand the forms you are using — by which I mean, if you manipulate form, space, and negative space in relation to other buildings or to the city in order to make compositional relationships — you can start to take over. If there was a hole in the ground where Notre Dame is today, and you had a church to build and you were really smart, you would make your church just like Notre Dame. The surrounding space is energized by the sculpture of that building and it co-opts a whole piece of Paris."[20]

Avoiding the limitations of a rationalized strategy of deconstruction, Frank Gehry makes incisions into the city fabric in an organic and intuitive manner. He may find on the site disparate objects, buildings, and structures built in different times in different styles and textures. In thinking intuitively and working with the materials at hand, he moves forward to bring into perspective a feeling of overall orientation, not necessarily in a sequential or systematic order, but by digression — in spurts and halts. And by breaking down the scale of the elements and adding new sculptural objects or basic, simple structures, he enters into different visual relationships, pictorial in a sense. It takes time to figure them out; they are never obvious but rather unfold by themselves, sometimes as seamlessly interwoven as the old and new in his Santa Monica home, in which a new, perforated structure, built in 1978, was virtually wrapped around the existing "gambrel-roofed bungalow," as Gehry calls it.

On July 13, 1991, around noon, with the architect back in his office, the three wavy, white paper scraps covering the Great Hall, represented by blocks on the Bilbao model, were unceremoniously discarded. The sculptural roof form, with sails acting as light scoops, was reworked into the imagery of a flower unfolding. The changes began with Gehry making three-dimensional sketches out of torn-up paper and blocks. Describing the process, he said, "Simultaneously I'm doing all these things, and I'm going nuts doing the drawings. I'm just ravenous. I'm flying and rushing back and forth, and then making these models, but nothing is going fast enough, and in the meantime I'm thinking of skylights for the atrium."

Guggenheim Museum Bilbao,
west elevation showing
skylights, July 13, 1991.
Ink on paper, 23 x 30.5 cm.

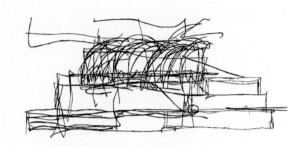

Guggenheim Museum Bilbao,
skylight designs, July 13, 1991.
Ink on paper, 23 x 30.5 cm.

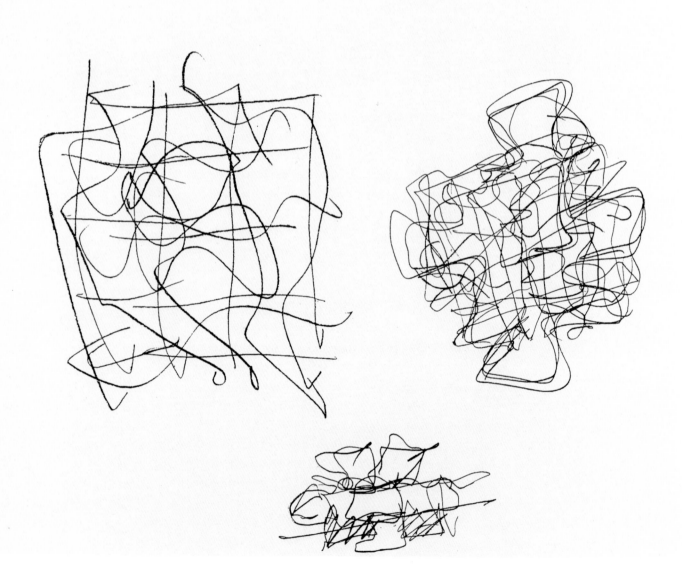

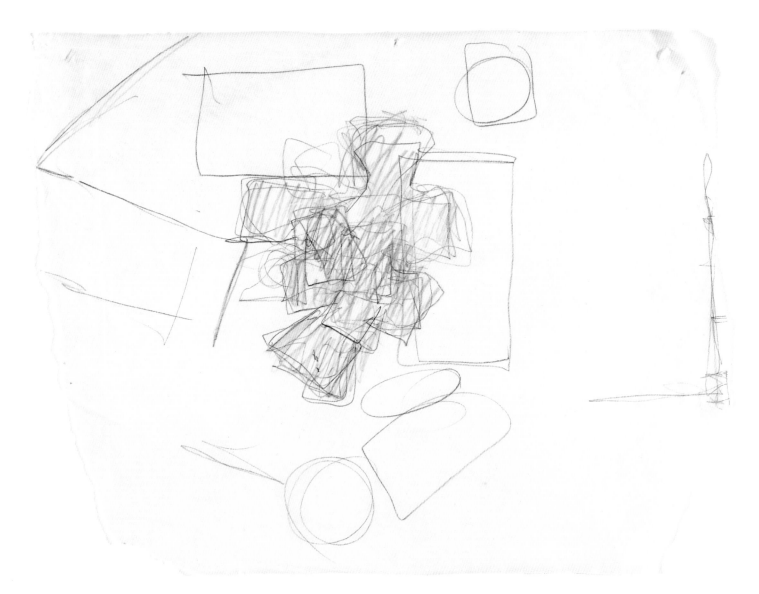

Guggenheim Museum Bilbao,
plan showing skylights,
July 13, 1991.
Colored pencil and pencil on
tracing paper, 35 x 44.5 cm.

The process of the transformation of the skylights is shown in three tracings: "I have a road map, and I know where I'm going. It frees me too, I decide where and how the pieces fit the site, determine the scale, and start a formal vocabulary, which I then can explain to somebody." Looking for a way to avoid the conventional approach — fenestration in squares for the glass surface of the skylights — Gehry drew curvilinear mullions. Another tracing, in view from above, elaborates on the skylights in the form of the unfolding flower. On the very top are two light scoops colored terra-cotta; the level below is made of a group of scoops colored green, covering among other things the entry; the warehouse-type building of the west elevation; the head piece of the gallery running underneath the bridge; and the area above a canopy, which is colored yellow to accentuate the lowest level.

The initial stage of skylights in the form of the flower was developed, as Chan recounted it, "within the course of a lunch hour," on July 13. In May 1991, Gehry had worked on a competition proposal for a new office tower for the Los Angeles Rapid Transit District (RTD); essentially, it consists of a traditional high-rise shape that, at its top, is radically distorted into a dynamic sculptural composition of undulating forms. The exterior was supposed to be stainless steel. In the midst of preparing for the imminent Bilbao competition, Gehry knew he could not take the time to refine his model, and as he suspected that the RTD project was too visionary to be realized, he felt that he could recycle the exuberant shape of the skyscraper top: "I took it, feeling that we would reinvent later. If we won, we'd come back with something else. I never thought we would continue with it."

Model for the Los Angeles Rapid Transit District tower (1991).

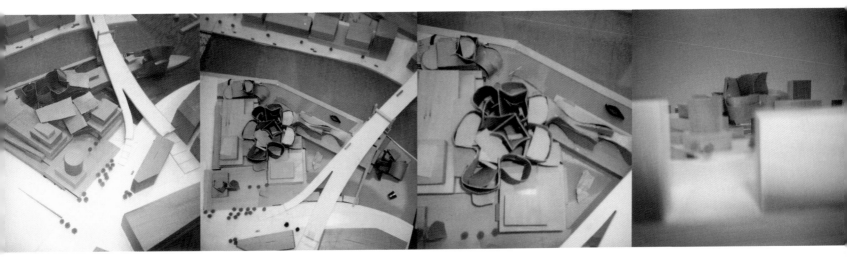

Polaroids showing the development of the Great Hall skylights, July 13, a.m. (far left) and July 15 (center left and right); and the view toward the Guggenheim Museum Bilbao along Calle de Iparraguirre, July 13, p.m.

The skylights in Bilbao were to be made out of metal, a material easy to modulate; like the RTD design, the skin of the building was to continue from the sides up to the top. Gehry set the proportions of the flower and its height in relation to the bridge and to the buildings surrounding the site. Polaroids were taken every day in order to show the trajectory of the thought process; keeping a record of the sequence of moves gave the architect the freedom to accelerate by jumping ahead intuitively rather than logically, while retaining the opportunity to backtrack. The series of Polaroids from July 13 through 15 shows the process of shaping the flower and other building components, such as the restaurant piece, shifting from limestone into the more fluid metal vocabulary.

Once the diagram of the flower-like skylights was more or less set, Gehry continued over the next two days to refine the individual forms; the pieces of Strathmore paper (sprayed with silver paint to represent metal) had been folded loosely around the basswood scraps representing light scoops, and therefore had taken on an amorphous look, so he tightened them: "I go out on a limb," Gehry said, "and then I get scared or something and I start to say, 'Wait a minute, there's a simpler way to do this.'" Realizing at the same time how strongly defined the sculptural element of the skylights was, he began to relate the "flower" to other parts of the building and to the cityscape surrounding it. On July 13, the architect himself took a Polaroid of the model as if viewed from the Alhóndiga, several blocks south of the museum, showing the flower clearly visible but fitting in scale into the neighborhood, to create a cognitive linkage.

below: Polaroids showing the placement of the bootlike shape on the north façade, July 13, a.m. (left) and July 13, p.m. (center); and a sail-like piece positioned as a base for the tower, July 13, a.m. (right).

facing page: Polaroids showing the development of the tower, July 13, p.m. (left), July 14, p.m. (center), and July 15, a.m. (right).

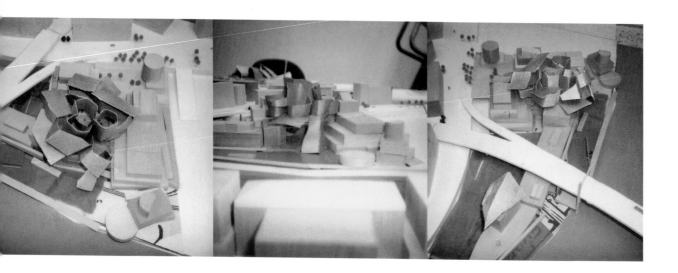

A piece of the flower, clad in silver-colored paper, was brought down and placed into the water garden; here, it took on a bootlike form. In a gestural move to enclose the skylight on top of the huge gallery, another piece began to relate the flower to the tower under development, while involving the bridge. A Polaroid taken the morning of July 13 shows that a leftover sail-like piece from the earlier design for the skylights, turned on its side and creatively interpreted as a boat form, was set onto a base as a start for the tower, only to be rejected the next day, when the architect seriously began to develop the tower design.

A sketch shows the long gallery being used as a pedestal for the tower structure, but the concept for the tower to be built in metal, with its forward-melting, sculptural base, ended up closely resembling the RTD tower. Once the flower and tower were in place, the west elevation followed. On July 15, the model was sufficiently developed to broadly show the direction Gehry would take with the museum; basswood pieces indicate the elements to be constructed in Spanish limestone, while silver-painted components represent metal. It only remained to give an impression of the interior of the Great Hall in some sketches.

The Jung Institute design and the Loyola Law School were architectural endeavors that represent a passive interchange between the urban environment and the site. In the Bilbao project, however, Gehry seized the chance to design not only a sculptural building, a museum with a strong iconic identity, but also a cynosure that would both energize the surrounding area and internalize the city within the different building components. At the time that the architect clarified his insight of takeover through the example of Notre Dame, he was about to start again on an intense process of refinement and redefinement of his design for the Bilbao Guggenheim: "I realized that this stuff was so arbitrary and so off the wall," Gehry said. "Why was I doing it? I was interested in the ten-day sketch, it was great, it was exciting, and then I became Mr. Architect."

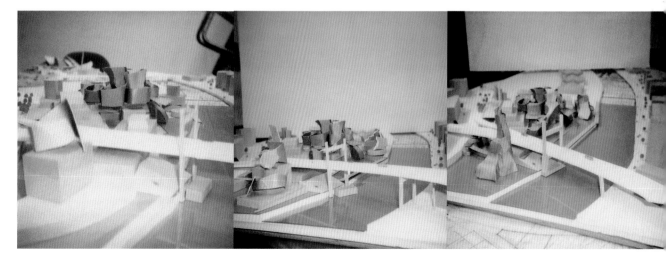

facing page and below: Guggenheim Museum Bilbao, north elevation, July 15, 1991.
Ink on paper, 23 x 30.5 cm.

right: Polaroid showing north elevation, July 15, a.m.

below left: Polaroid showing west elevation, July 13, p.m.

below right: Guggenheim Museum Bilbao, west elevation, July 13, 1991, p.m.
Ink on paper, 23 x 30.5 cm.

facing page: Guggenheim Museum Bilbao, west elevation, July 15, 1991.
Ink on paper, 23 x 30.5 cm.

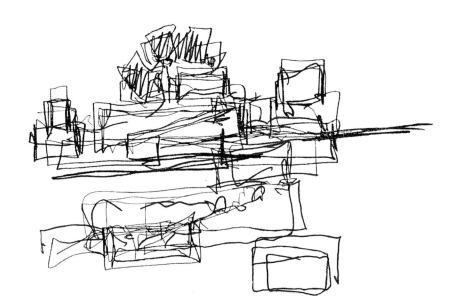

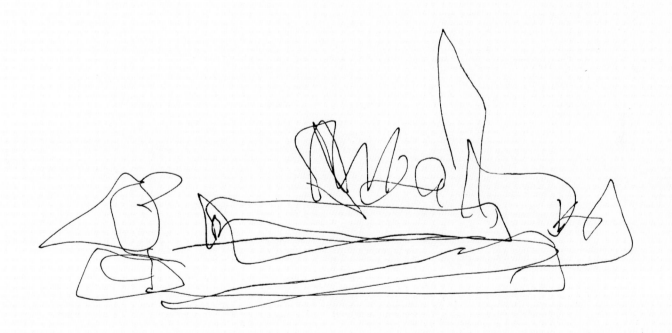

above: Guggenheim Museum Bilbao, tower elevation, July 14, 1991, p.m. Ink on paper, 23 x 30.5 cm.

below left: Polaroid showing tower development, July 14, p.m.

below right: Polaroid showing tower development, July 15, a.m.

facing page: Guggenheim Museum Bilbao, views of tower, July 14, 1991, a.m. Ink on paper, 23 x 30.5 cm.

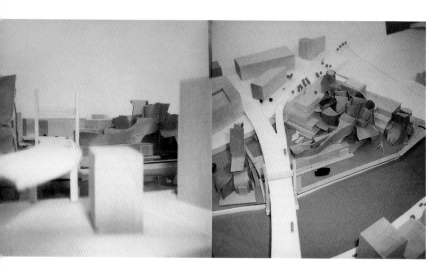

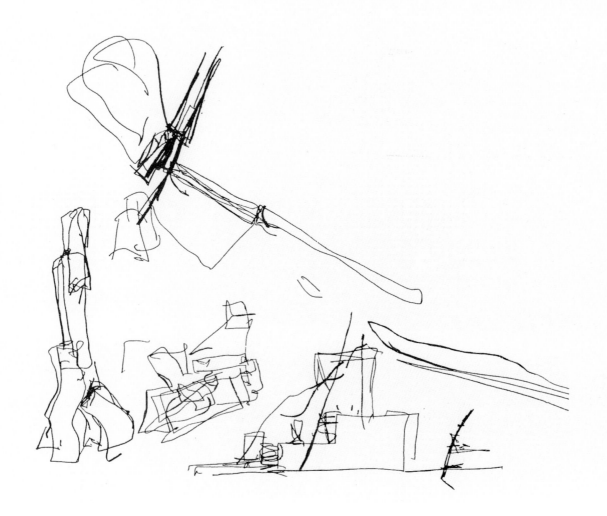

facing page: Guggenheim Museum Bilbao, interior view of the Great Hall, July 16, 1991. Ink on tracing paper, 52.1 x 43.2 cm.

below: Guggenheim Museum Bilbao, north elevation showing the Great Hall, July 16, 1991. Ink on paper, 23 x 30.5 cm.

Polaroids showing completed schematic model, July 15.

Model parts on the wall of Gehry's Santa Monica studio, 1994.

Toward a Unity of Opposites: A Mere Building Versus Sculptural Architecture

I have been fortunate to have had support from living painters and sculptors. I have never felt that what artists are doing is very different. I have always felt there is a moment of truth when you decide: what color, what size, what composition? How you get to that moment of truth is different and the end result is different.

Solving all the functional problems is an intellectual exercise. That is a different part of my brain. It's not less important, it's just different. And I make a value out of solving all those problems, dealing with the context and the client and finding my moment of truth after I understand the problem.[21]

Frank Gehry

On August 3, 1991, some two weeks after Frank O. Gehry and Associates had won the competition for the Guggenheim Museum Bilbao, Krens sent a letter to the architect, "written in haste," in which he summed up the positives and negatives of the scheme as observed by the architectural-review committee. Gehry's use of materials characteristic of the industrial site, such as steel and mortar, was favorably perceived, as was the bringing in of water onto the platform. The committee commented that the museum noticeably interacted with its visitors "on a number of interior and exterior planes, such as plazas, vistas, fountains etc." The letter stated, furthermore, that the committee liked the potential for fairly simple large exhibition spaces and the concept of "the rotunda with its resources and echoes with the Guggenheim in New York and in Salzburg." Most of all, they liked the engagement with the bridge and the linkage to the "waterfront/port environment."

A subject of controversy was the high reader in the form of a tower. Discussions circled around the questions of whether the tower should have a function, whether it might be too excessive in scale, or whether such a dominant presence was desirable at all. Other concerns emerged in the letter. It was not clear from the model where exactly the entrance to the museum would be. In addition, Krens wrote that "the sandblasted steel element was seen as a sculptural bonnet on top of rational and regular exhibition spaces." While some committee members saw this as "a brilliant solution to more systematically forcing the overall spatial architecture of the building into contortions, thereby negatively impacting the art inside the space" — the Guggenheim Wright building often cited as a case in point — they all felt that the "sculptural bonnet," visibly the most distinctive component of the building, should be refined. The committee also expressed its opinion that the involvement of "site sculpture, while laudable, was entirely out of scale with the sculpture of the building." Finally, as was to be expected given the short time span of the competition, the "interrelationships between the different types of gallery spaces, special exhibitions, the encyclopedic collection, and spaces dedicated to ten specific artists" needed further attention.

As a client, Krens was ready to partake in all development stages of the project. He commissioned a feasibility study, conducted by three Spanish firms, GESTEC, IBS S.A., and KPMG Peat Marwick, and published by the Solomon R. Guggenheim Foundation in 1992, which included art programming and management services needed, a demographic and economic-impact analysis, and an engineering and technical-cost estimate. Krens also had a vision of how the Guggenheim Museum Bilbao was to fit into the conglomerate of other Guggenheim museums, as related in the interview of February 1997: "I conceive the Guggenheim Museum as one museum that has a constellation of spaces.... Some stars in the firmament might burn a little bit brighter — but that's what constellations are all about.... If you look at the constellation of these spaces, the Frank Lloyd Wright building is a stand-alone building; the Peggy Guggenheim Collection [in Venice] is a converted private house, just as MASS MoCA is a converted factory space.... To come back to the Frank Gehry building, it is the apotheosis of the stand-alone building. The complete reverse of that, from an architectural standpoint, is Hans Hollein's building for Salzburg, which is invisible. I mean, it has no exterior presence, it

BILBAO . AUG 91

161 . SKETCHES .   F. GEHRY

facing page: Guggenheim Museum Bilbao, north elevation, August 1991.
Ink on paper, 23 x 30.5 cm.

below: The tower under construction, June 1997.

is pure interiority, and I think that that was spectacular. The last piece was a project that we were designing for Tokyo on top of a skyscraper."

Krens's objective is that each of these museum spaces, because of their specific identity, shape, and history, be suited to showing "some art rather than others," expressing the spirit and unique character of each place. This approach has led to certain site-specific commissions, such as Richard Serra's *Snake*, situated in the long boat-shaped gallery of the Bilbao Guggenheim. Another example of such a space is the one that the Solomon R. Guggenheim Foundation, in collaboration with the Deutsche Bank AG, will open in November 1997 on the recently restored ground floor of the 1920s headquarters of the Bank, situated on Unter den Linden in Berlin. The Deutsche Guggenheim Berlin will occupy 2,200 square meters; according to Krens, its main purpose is the commissioning of new works in an "unusual scale." He envisages the museum "playing an active role as a generator of culture and of art by creating the conditions"; the museum functioning "as Petri dish and the artist as fruit fly." What might be taken as an updated version of Edgar Allan Poe's comparison of the artist's yearning for the sublime to "the desire of the moth for the star," is also a continuation of the approach of the international Kunsthalle, which typically juxtaposes a grandiose installation by an individual artist with small, highly focused exhibits. The Dia Center for the Arts provides such a precedent for the systematic commissioning of new works — in 1977, for example, it commissioned Walter de Maria's *The New York Earthroom*, permanently installed in a space on Wooster Street in downtown New York City.

Gehry, meanwhile, continued to sketch, partly in reaction to the comments he had received. One sketch, dated August 1991, shows the riverside elevation with the flower configuration and a prominent canopy over the large glass wall of the atrium facing out over the Nervión River, as well as the boot-shaped gallery. A pile of stone pieces in front of the long gallery and just underneath the bridge have replaced the outdoor amphitheater; the Gehry team would refer to the pile as the "logjam," which would be the starting point of several

building components yet to be designed. Krens had felt that "under bridges, under culverts, it just doesn't work. Forget about it. You can walk past it, but there's just nothing you can do architecturally to make it attractive." But Gehry hoped to reclaim the negative area underneath the bridge, essential to the creation of a connection to the tower. At the request of the Bilbao city planner, Ibon Areso, he also incorporated into the design an extension of the walking path along the riverfront underneath the bridge.

In an August 30 letter, Krens asked Gehry to prepare a more elaborate model in the scale of 1:200, augmented with a larger contextual urban area in order to show the scale of the surrounding buildings, including the height of the bridge and "where it anchors to the opposite side of the river, and enough of the far side of the river to show the incline of the hill." This model would be presented to the Basque planning officials and the Guggenheim Board of Trustees in mid-September in New York. At the beginning of the project, Krens initiated an intensive dialogue with Gehry, marked by frequent visits to the architect's office in Los Angeles. He established a design rhythm by meeting Gehry and his project team twice a month, often without the involvement of the Basque participants: "I would take an 8:00 A.M. flight in the morning from Kennedy, get to Los Angeles at 11:00 A.M. We would work all day, and then I'd come back to New York either at 4:00 A.M. or 11:00 the next morning."

The Basque team rarely interceded in the design requirements or building specifications; they would respond to Gehry's questions about details, such as the maximum flood line, but, as Krens stated, "they were witnesses. They were there as managers of the future construction project; they were there as cost estimators and contractors. But they were not necessarily there for their design input. So therefore we had what was almost a free hand . . . only restrained by the 256,000 square foot [24,000 square meters] limitation and the budget [$100 million]." Once the budget was approved by the Basque Administration, Juan Ignacio Vidarte, then Director of the Consorcio — the Basque group managing the building and planning of the project — made sure that everybody stayed within it. This firm stance had an important impact on the overall design, which had to be redefined several times because of budget restrictions. Vidarte stuck consistently to what he considered the "initial set of rules," which comprised a clear "division of labor": "Don't hinder the design, which was Gehry's realm, nor force his hand." At the same time, he approved of the creative relationship between Krens and Gehry, and felt that the end result could only benefit from Krens's museum expertise.

In August and again in October 1991, Gehry made more sketches searching for an articulation of the atrium in terms of its function and sculptural presence. At this time, the interior is defined by the same two ziggurats as in the competition phase, one on the south and one on the west side, with ramps descending into the center. Gehry seems to have been occupied with the circulation flow, as evidenced by supplemental notations referring to two other projects: in the upper-left corner of the sheet is drawn a concise ground plan, reminiscent of the Walt Disney Concert Hall, consisting of a box with lobbies, and other spaces around its perimeter, and in the lower-right corner a simpler version of a box with sculptural addition at its corner, identifiable as the scheme of the Vitra factory in Weil am Rhein, Germany.

Guggenheim Museum Bilbao, north elevation showing atrium (center)
and annotations, August 1991. Ink on paper, 23 x 30.5 cm.

F. Gehry   Oct./91

Guggenheim Museum Bilbao, north elevations, October 1991.
Ink on paper, 23 x 30.5 cm.

In the second sketch, the image of the atrium, ethereal and in flux, rendered by continuous contours, appears in a wonderful composition of three horizontal images: the top and bottom show the essential components of the complete river elevation; between them is the same view, but seen from the long gallery, with the sweeping skylight on its top up to the bootlike gallery. The ziggurat is absent, because Gehry ran out of space at the edge of the sheet. This time he arrived at an understanding of the atrium by clarifying its scale, expressed as a tighter, more roomlike enclosure. "I start drawing sometimes," he recently said, "not knowing exactly where it is going. I use familiar strokes that evolve into the building, which I'm prone to sketching.... Sometimes it seems directionless, not going anywhere for sure. It's like feeling your way along in the dark, anticipating that something will come out usually. I become a voyeur of my own thoughts as they develop, and wander about them. Sometimes I say 'boy, here it is, here it is, it's coming.' I understand it. I get all excited and from there I'll move to the models, and the models drain all the energy, and need information on scale and relationships that you can't conceive in totality in drawings. The drawings are ephemeral. The models are the specific; they then become like sketches in the next phase."

Gehry aspires to engage people in a physical manner in his buildings, through refraction of the building components into human scale, issues of comfort, and the application of tactile materials. Conceptualization is easier in a small-scale model, which, placed on a lazy Susan in order to be perceived from all viewpoints, is treated more like a sculpture. The drawback, though, according to Gehry is "becoming complacent. You forget about it as architecture, because you're focused on this sculpting process." By going back and forth between different scales the architect is jolted into thinking about the project's actual dimensions: "I'm always looking at eye level, I'm always thinking of what the space is like. And by shifting the scale, it forces me out of the fascination with the model as it is. The reality of the model is a fiction, it's not real, it's only a tool for the final building."

Gehry has an even more ingrained suspicion of the seductive qualities of architectural render-ings, the glib representations of projects as sales products for a client. Before he started his own practice in Los Angeles, he made renderings to earn a living. Taught by Carlos Diniz, a professional renderer, Gehry managed to draw perspective accurately, and trees, but never people. However, rendering did not satisfy him: "I felt that I could seduce myself into believ-ing that something was good by a good rendering or drawing. And I rejected it all. I used to have a structural engineer redraw my ideas so that I had to fight the dry character of the drawings to get the essence of the project without the seductiveness. During that period, the mid-1960s, I started to sketch for myself." Realizing that architectural renderings are stylized and artificial, Gehry prefers to move into models in the development stages of a project. Once these, in turn, become sketchlike and free, he tends to stop sketching. However, "often the models take me down a blind alley, and I go back to sketches again. They become the vehicle for propelling the project forward when I get stuck."

Functional problems of the building are worked out in schematic models in which pragmatic solutions to the building prevail over aesthetic decisions, followed by sculptural study models to and fro leading up to the final scheme. Six main models of the Bilbao project sum-marize the development phase: 1) the sculptural competition model in a scale of 1:500, made of basswood and paper; 2) the presentation model, requested by Krens, in a scale of 1:200, made of plaster and metal; shown to the Board of Trustees of the Solomon R. Guggenheim Foundation and the Basque officials in New York on September 16, 1991, it was basically a cleaned up version of the competition model; 3) the schematic design model, in a scale of 1:200, made of wood and metal, finished in February 1993; 4) the schematic model shown at the occasion of the groundbreaking of the Guggenheim Museum Bilbao on October 20, 1993, in a scale of 1:200, made of wood and paper; 5) the design model, in a scale of 1:100, made of basswood and paper that Gehry was working on all along from the fall of 1992 until December 1993; and, 6) in February 1994, a verification model in a scale of 1:100, whose refined, computer-generated shapes derived from the design model were milled out of an

facing page and above, left to right:
Presentation model in plaster and
metal shown to the Solomon R.
Guggenheim Foundation's Board
of Trustees and Basque officials in
New York, September 16, 1991;
schematic design model in wood
and metal, completed February
1993; schematic model in wood
and paper shown at groundbreaking ceremonies in Bilbao on
October 20, 1993; design model
in basswood and paper that Gehry
worked on from fall 1992 to
December 1993.

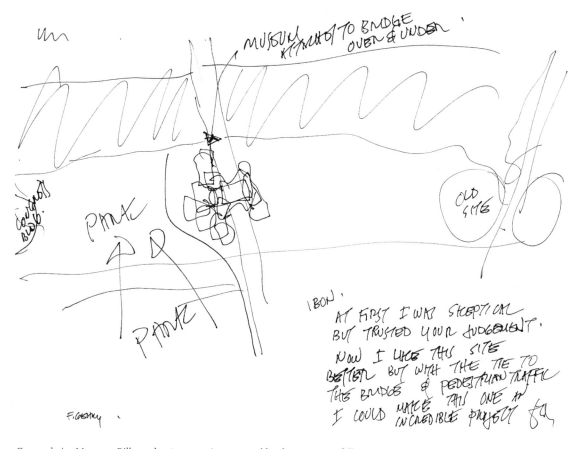

Guggenheim Museum Bilbao, plan (on new site proposed by Ibon Areso in fall 1992),
late fall 1992. Ink on paper, 23 x 30.5 cm.

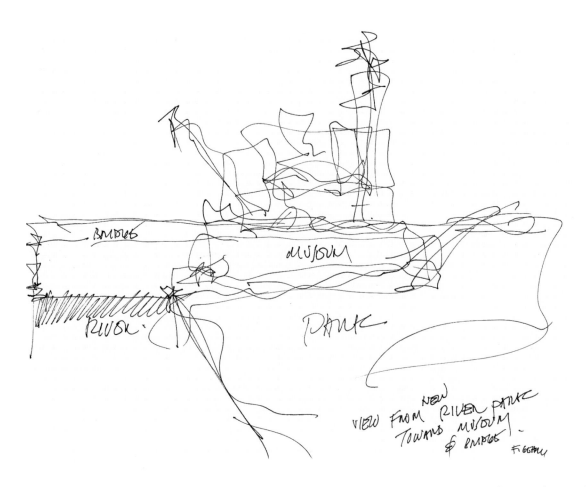

Guggenheim Museum Bilbao, west elevation (on new site proposed by Ibon Areso in fall 1992), late fall 1992. Ink on paper, 23 x 30.5 cm.

industrial foam representing metal and wood blocks standing in for Spanish limestone. From February 1994, several additional models of interior galleries in a scale of 1:25 were built; one, for instance, was made of the block containing the interior spaces of the six classical galleries, in order to study the custom light fixtures.

By late fall 1992, as a result of the feasibility study, the amount of square meters the new museum would occupy had been diminished by one third — from 36,000 square meters to 24,000 square meters, and eventually increased again to 28,500 square meters — while the desirable ratio of galleries to facilities, such as storage, retail, restaurant, and so on, stayed roughly the same. The reduction of space became a liberating incentive for Gehry to question his competition scheme freely, and not only to rethink the project but, if necessary, to start from scratch. At that particular moment it happened that Areso, the Bilbao city planner, sent him a proposal to move the museum one bridge to the west, closer to the Museo de Bellas Artes, with the Universidad de Deusto across the river. It is remarkable how little fixated Gehry was on his original scheme; he understood the interesting urbanistic potential of bringing together the Guggenheim Museum Bilbao and, next to it, a projected Congress Hall, as gateways to the older part of the city to the south, surrounded by a park extending toward the river. The museum could involve the bridge from above and below, with pedestrians and traffic literally moving through it, which would make the building completely accessible not only

Guggenheim Museum Bilbao,
plan, December 1992.
Ink on paper, 23 x 30.5 cm.

Guggenheim Museum Bilbao,
plan (top) and tower elevation
(bottom), late fall 1992.
Ink on paper, 23 x 30.5 cm.

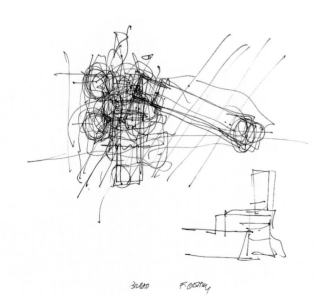

to museum visitors but to all the people of Bilbao. A model was initiated, but soon thereafter the new concept, while tempting, was abandoned.

After this detour, the Bilbao project was seriously scrutinized, then put back on its former course. In late fall 1992, Gehry made a series of four sketches, reexamining urban relationships, unraveling and rearranging building elements. One sketch shows a reinterpretation of the long gallery as a big square space; in the center of the atrium, two ziggurats are placed next to one another. In another sketch, the west elevation with ziggurat and ramp facing the industrial area no longer consists of a long wall as in the competition model, but is replaced by two sculptural rounded accents, still unresolved. The museum entrance runs more diagonally in relation to the existing street. A long building with a small sculptural accent, which would eventually become a blue office building, breaks down the large scale in order to conform to the neighboring buildings, and runs straight into the atrium, eliminating the ziggurat. The long gallery is projected underneath the bridge, ending in a sculptural accent on its other side, to be turned into a tower. A notation in the lower-right corner elaborates on how the tower is situated on top of and attached to the long gallery.

Guggenheim Museum Bilbao,
skylight (top left), north elevation
(top right), plan (bottom left),
and skylight details (bottom
right), late fall 1992.
Ink on paper, 23 x 30.5 cm.

The disagreements about the scheme of the building were resolved in a charette that lasted from Thanksgiving through Christmas of 1992. A final overall scheme was worked out that contained three concentrically located, rectilinear galleries radiating out from the atrium. One of the galleries replaces the sculptural accents on the west elevation. For the first time, the long gallery becomes curved like a boat form, as shown in the river view situated at the top of the sheet. In the upper-left corner, the skylight on top of the boat gallery is drawn instead of an isolated "bonnet" on top of the atrium. In accordance with the reduced program, the idea became to contain the energy and compress the scheme into a dense urban experience. The boot-shaped gallery descends from the flower and extends into the water garden; next to it is a tightened atrium with a pronounced canopy, and a sculptural accent on the other side of the boot-shaped gallery, which would become integrated eventually as the riverfront gallery.

Guggenheim Museum Bilbao,
north elevation, July 1992.
Ink on paper, 23 x 30.5 cm.

Finally, in this new scheme, leaflike contours of galleries begin to engage the rectangular building components.

Krens had insisted upon different types of galleries, some sculptural, with six more classical, rectilinear ones; Gehry's team nicknamed these the "stodgy" galleries. Krens's argument was that "the visceral and psychological experience of the building was like that of an opera," but to "just have a constantly loud crescendo taking place all the time was too much. [Gehry] needed to vary the rhythm of the thing, number one, and we also had to create what sparked that. There is a logic for galleries being rectilinear. I mean, there's an efficiency about it that has to do with the fact that we walk upright and that the paintings hang on the wall." The permanent walls required for the classical galleries create a kind of rigidity, but Krens felt that "a building needs discipline from time to time.... You don't create an aircraft hangar every time you want to do something.... So it was discipline and contrast."

Gehry listened carefully to Krens, accepted the 4 meter high walls he proposed, adding a vaultlike space on the top level, and over time synthesized other requests, including wider skylights and, in the center of the rectilinear galleries, which would have two levels each, open shafts running through, in order to create a natural light source. The only aesthetic principle the architect would not deviate from was that in the final outcome this classical white box had to become part of the building as a whole, seamlessly interwoven and juxtaposed with the sculpturally shaped galleries, resulting in a unity of opposites, the rigor of the geometric combined with the fluidity of the organic.

While the overall scheme for the museum had been decided upon during the charette, it remained for the project team to work out the details. Gehry and Chan set out to redesign the flower configuration and the atrium, a task that would occupy them respectively until October 1993 and fall 1994. It would even take through March 1995 to complete the tower design. Gehry had begun to wonder "what [the flower configuration] had to do with art, and whether it had to do with this museum," he recalled in November 1996. He also remembered the following episode: "I came to Krens's office and Richard Serra was there, and Michael Govan [former Deputy Director of the Guggenheim]. They were talking about Boccioni, and

Model showing interior of classical galleries, 1993.

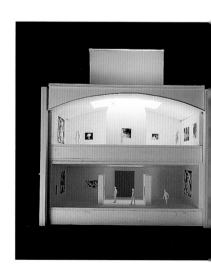

that they thought it came from Boccioni.... I'd seen Boccioni, but it wasn't something I would get excited about, so I think that was an accidental reading."

Of course, when one thinks of Umberto Boccioni's bronze sculptures, particularly *Development of a Bottle in Space* (1912), which is so architectonic in character, there do seem to be correspondences between Boccioni's version of the *élan vital*, based upon the Bergsonian principle of duration, and Gehry's strategy of an all-pervading energy flow. Analogies can be drawn between leaps in the scale of Boccioni's bottle and Gehry's flower to building components, between, in Boccioni, the spiraling movement into planes through an abstracted reconstruction of the object and, in Gehry, the manipulation of sculptural masses on the basis of straight line segments. But Boccioni broke up the object through redistribution of its parts starting from its core, extending its plasticity into space with a spiraling, dynamic tension. Gehry, on the other hand, let his flower unfold in disparate elements, spreading sideways and downward in a fluid motion, echoing the flux of the river and flow of the surrounding traffic, and ultimately resonating in leaflike galleries interwoven with geometric building elements.

Boccioni sought "to *abolish in sculpture*, as in all arts, the traditionally *'sublime' subject matter*," as he stated in his *Technical Manifesto of Futurist Sculpture* (1912). Gehry, more ambiguously, took the configuration of a flower, which in the predominantly Catholic Basque country cannot but have overtones of a sublime symbol of divinity, the rose of the Virgin Mary, shifted its context, and, by displacing it from cathedral to museum, made it a comment in itself. At the same time, by individualizing the design of its configuration, which had to adhere to the logical placement of functional skylights for galleries, and by executing the flower in an industrial material, titanium, he ended up with a demythologized, emotive, mnemonic image, no longer incisive, but evanescent. Gehry's flower form, as adornment on top of the RTD headquarters, might have become, in Frank Lloyd Wright's words, a "Gothic-commercial competitor" to the church spire, but atop the atrium of the Guggenheim Museum Bilbao the flower configuration unfolds into a transient sign of our times, eluding meaning and remaining an enigma.

Revised model with a square atrium and galleries in place of the flowerlike skylight shapes, late fall 1992.

To return to the final design stages, by December 1992, Gehry was especially aware of the jarring relationship between the exterior and interior of the flower. Moreover, the entire atrium was in need of clarification; Krens had commented that its scheme of different wall levels resulting from stepped ziggurats projecting into the space — from which paintings or video screens were to be suspended — reminded him of a "hotel lobby." In search of a principle joining the elements, Gehry started in a radical way by reducing the flowerlike shapes of the skylights to purely functional squares. Next, he turned the atrium itself into a square, and filled it with a series of square galleries. "I didn't expect to do this, I was just trying to find a way back," Gehry recollected in a November 1996 interview. "I always go back to a base of rectangles and boxes and the simplest idea, look at it, and then distort again from it." Krens, who happened to come by the office, unequivocally rejected the revised design. The architect remembered him saying, "I don't want any of that. Think of Frank Lloyd Wright's rotunda. People hate it or love it; Flavin did an installation there, Calder looked good in there, and when you have living artists, they'll react to it."

Krens's response brought back to Gehry a discussion he had about museums with the conceptual artist Daniel Buren some fifteen years earlier.[22] He stated at the time, "My typical stance has been that the museum should be laid-back and a simple box, in which the artist can come and do anything," expecting that, because he was deferential to the arts, he would be approved of as "a nice, polite architect." To Gehry's surprise, Buren reacted differently. "In case you involve yourself in such a thing one day … make the best building you can do. I think to try to make simple, neutral space would be the worst way. For what?" In turning the atrium into galleries, Gehry's inclination had been to yield to art, but, as Krens, in February 1997, recalled telling him, "it simply was not necessary to create exhibition space in the atrium. This atrium is yours, you're the artist here. This is your sculpture … you then make perfect exhibition spaces around it." Krens urged Gehry to focus on the creation of a central dramatic space from which the circulation to the galleries would originate and to which it would return. As for the galleries, they should be adaptable to a wide range of art. As he phrased it, "The idea was that the museum had to be able to accommodate the biggest and heaviest of any existing contemporary sculpture on the one hand, and a Picasso drawing on the other hand."

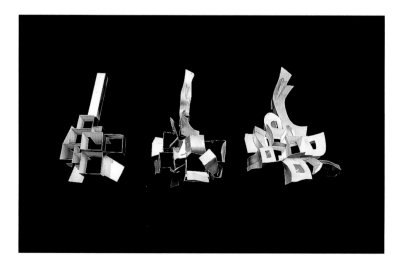

Model parts, studies of the atrium
exterior, September 1992.

Once Gehry realized that the flower configuration needed only to cover the atrium, and not spill out over other galleries, he pulled it back into a constrained composition. This move led him to a transformation of the scheme into three galleries radiating from the atrium, vaguely leaflike in their contours, shifting into echoes of nautical and truncated fish imagery. One became located along the riverfront next to the bootlike gallery, another in between the entry ramp and the geometric building components housing the six classical galleries, and the third began to engage the other side of it. Next, the flower configuration on top of the atrium was widened, at the same time as the atrium itself became compressed.

Gehry often finds his inspiration beyond architecture, in art. In giving an example, he said: "On this building I looked a lot at the cutouts of Matisse, at these big, long shapes just casually cut ... the awkwardness of them." The cutouts suggested that the boat gallery, and the three leaflike galleries, having gone through an endless process of refining the same shapes, needed that sense of awkwardness, giving the effect of a more casual disposition of form. In addition, "the mutation of architecture into sculpture" has enticed Gehry as well, as exemplified in his own fish and snake designs. In 1990, while designing the Chiat/Day office building in Venice, the architect had come up with a solution to the façade by inserting in the

Chiat/Day office building, Venice, California (1991).

One of the leaflike galleries in the Guggenheim Museum Bilbao, July 1997.

Nationale-Nederlanden office building, Prague (1996).

center of the model another small model, by Claes Oldenburg, of a building in the form of binoculars, which the artist had left in the office. Through this act, Gehry turned what might well have remained an unfeasible project into a collaboration, in which the *Binoculars* became an integral part of his building, yet were separate enough to stand on their own.

Gehry has never avoided memorable images from artists he respects. He fictionalizes the process as a "communal game": "Whoever is playing puts an idea on the table; the parlay from the *London Knees* [a multiple by Oldenburg] to Prague [Gehry's Nationale-Nederlanden office building] to Richard [Serra]'s new pieces is amazing. Richard says that he was influenced by the Lewis residence, and it's obvious I was influenced by the *Knees*, although I didn't know it. Everybody sees it, [Frank] Stella saw it. So I look at it as a communal language." With Krens backing him fully, Gehry's moment had come to freely cross over to and fro between architecture and sculpture in his design for the atrium of the Guggenheim Bilbao. As he expressed it, "part of me wanted to be discovered."

Gehry realizes all too well that he is pushing at the parameters of an architecture, boxed in by set rules: "To say that a building has to have a certain kind of architectural attitude to be a building is too limiting, so the best thing to do is to make the sculptural functional in terms of use. If you can translate the beauty of sculpture into the building…whatever it does to give movement and feeling, that's where the innovation in architecture is." And to him, it was Le Corbusier who explored innovation in materials and techniques "in a plastic sense beyond architecture, taking it out of its limits."

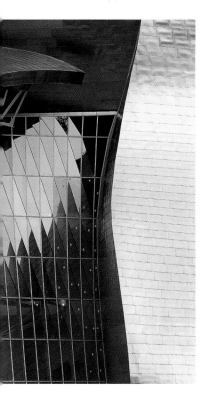

Guggenheim Museum Bilbao, curtain-wall glazing leading to atrium, July 1997.

In the atrium design, Gehry started out with the complexities inherent in architecture of what functionally had to be: two elevators and two stair banks, mechanical shafts and catwalks. The space at the top had to be raised one third higher for the restored flower configuration, a move determined by its proportion in relation to the surrounding buildings and the bridge. Thus, from a distance, the Guggenheim Bilbao could blend into the urban landscape, even though close up it would feel larger than life. Thinking about the mechanics of how to direct the flow of people to and from the galleries, and envisioning at the end of the gallery space on the second-floor level a balcony as a lookout on the city, evoked visionary urban designs, such as Antonio Sant'Elia's The New City, but even more persistent were images from Fritz Lang's 1926 film *Metropolis*. Gehry liked the idea of creating a central place indoors as a metaphor for the ideal modern city, into which artists could put pieces and capture the space, an impossibility if situated in the actual cityscape, where outdoor sculpture always is dwarfed by the environment.

The interstices, which consist of shaped curtain-wall glazing, fill the cracks between the concentrically laid-out galleries and the continuation of the entry ramps running into the atrium. These, together with the large windowlike opening facing the waterfront — also comprised of different glazed shapes — create a way to interact with the city. For instance, standing inside the atrium space, one can see oneself in relation to a fraction of the huge skylight on top of the boat gallery, and a piece of the Puente de la Salve all at once. Turning around, one catches a glimpse through the entry of the buildings along the Alameda de Mazarredo; in the opposite

Constantin Brancusi's Paris studio.

Guggenheim Museum Bilbao, views of the atrium in models and the finished building.

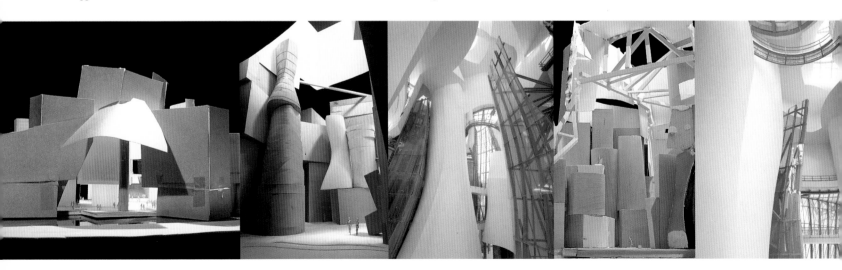

direction one overlooks a corner of the Universidad de Deusto across the Nervión River. At the same time, the interstitial curtain-wall glazings function as negatives of sculptural elements disposed vertically around the periphery of the atrium's interior, such as three rectangular twisted limestone obelisks housing mechanical equipment; two elevator towers, one in glass the other in plaster; two stair towers, one in glass and the other in plaster; a plaster tower with niche; and a plaster support column.

The dense overlay of positive and negative shapes partly eclipsing one another results in a strong visual dynamic of ever-changing forms. Despite the overwhelming height, Gehry felt that, standing in the atrium space, one should experience more the informality of a crowded, rough-textured sculptor's studio, something like that of Brancusi's legendary Paris studio, filled with a multitude of works in different scales and materials. He perceives such an organically evolved environment of ideal forms in chance relationships as a prototype for urbanistic design: "[Brancusi's studio] looked like a whole city.... The idealistic city, though I don't think he intended that." Although obelisks, pillars, and towers, all shooting up to the very top

of the atrium to merge visually with the plaster sculptural roof form, from whose glazed openings the interior is flooded with light, contribute to an intensification of verticals as if in a Gothic cathedral, this upward thrust disperses into the exterior flower, unfolding, disconnecting into leaflike galleries, flowing sideways over the boat gallery, and dissipating downward into the water garden from the bootlike gallery, the whole unified by the application of the shimmering aeronautical material, titanium.

One component of the Guggenheim Bilbao — the tower on the other side of the Puente de la Salve — still remained to be solved. The tower lacked a function, and only limited funds were left for it. For budget reasons, the tower already could contain no more than one flight of stairs leading up to the deck level of the bridge. In a lecture given in spring 1997, the architect recollected proposing a postponement of the construction in order not to exceed $100 million dollars, and at the same time change the limestone to plaster for the office buildings and classical galleries in order to save money. But these proposals did not go over well with Vidarte and his team: "I hit my first brick Basque wall," Gehry said. Their response was that the competition model had indicated stone as a material to be applied, and that it had included a tower, both of which should stay part of the building.

The tower development, begun in the competition model as a sculptural shape melting forward at its base — an idea reminiscent of the RTD skyscraper design — eventually had become interconnected with the "logjam" stone pieces shown in the August 1991 sketch and represented by wooden blocks on the model. These were left in place "to at least be in my conscience that I had to do something," Gehry recollected. "Finally I said, it looks like the river flew up in a bunch of containers, so I accepted it." In the follow-up, the two "logjam" components were made into café and storage spaces to be built in limestone, and located partly underneath the bridge adjacent to a ramp. The huge skylight flying toward the bridge on top of the boat gallery, together with the rising tower on the other side and the "logjam" pieces with the ramp, create a formally complementary relationship, and a programmatic one as well. All provide a way to reach the deck of the bridge. One can emerge from the tower onto the bridge deck, or descend from it to the riverfront, engaging with the city.

Gehry contemplated for a while an open mesh form like the Barcelona fish; then a glass tower; next a combination of a limestone-and-metal tower with a restaurant and terrace in its top, which Krens rejected. He offered to put a gallery space in it, but that was also turned down. For one week, he thought of a stone tower with a wire structure, but none of the designs was satisfactory. A breakthrough came in late fall 1994, when the tower came to be seen as an autonomic sculptural element. Clad in titanium, as in the competition model, the high reader seemed too much a mimicry of the flower configuration overwhelming it; changed to limestone, the tower, done in simple curves and long planes, and split with its inner steel structure showing, began to relate both to the existing buildings in the vicinity of the site and to the new office buildings and classical galleries. Suggestive of functional architecture, yet a pseudosculptural form, the afunctional tower had come into its own, "mutating" from architecture into sculpture, and back again.

View of model showing the "logjam," the cubic and cylindrical forms that appear to tumble from beneath the bridge, 1993.

The tower as it appeared in the competition model, July 1991.

The tower as it appeared in the presentation model shown to the Solomon R.
Guggenheim Foundation's Board of Trustees and Basque officials in New York,
September 16, 1991.

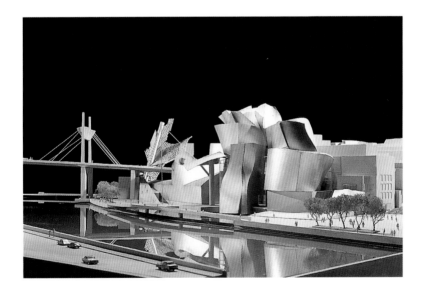

Polaroid showing the tower as it appeared in the schematic design model completed in February 1993.

The tower as it appeared in the schematic model shown at the groundbreaking ceremonies in Bilbao on October 20, 1993.

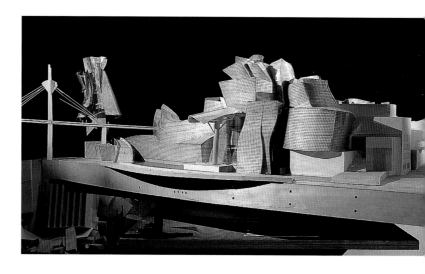

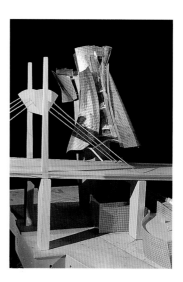

The tower as it appeared in the design model that Gehry worked on from fall 1992 to December 1993.

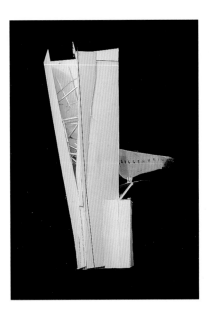

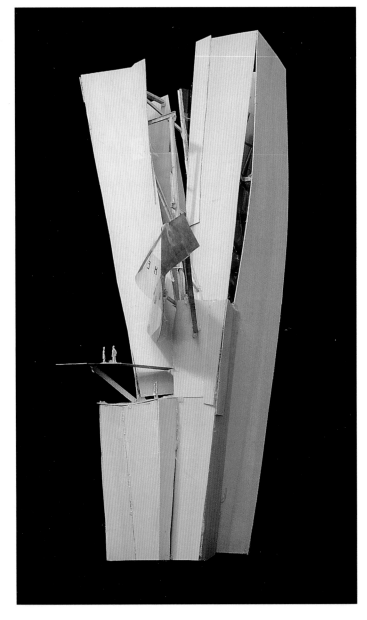

top left, above and right: The tower as it appeared in the final model, February 1994.

top right: The tower, November 1997.

The Guggenheim Museum Bilbao enacts an unfolding process of design. As its architect, Frank Owen Gehry says, it has had nothing to do with the magical bicycle trick, "hey ma, no hands." Instead, he sees the process from first sketch into building as an evolution: "In the first sketch I put a bunch of principles down. Then I become self-critical of those images and those principles, and they evoke the next set of responses. And as each piece unfolds, I make the models bigger, and bigger, bringing into focus more elements and more pieces of the puzzle. And once I have the beginning, a toehold into where I'm going, then I want to examine the parts in more detail. And those evolve, and at some point I stop, because that's it. I don't come to a conclusion, but I think there's a certain reality of pressures to get the thing done that I accept. It's maturity, or whatever you want to call it, to say, stop, go, finish. I've got other ideas now, and the door is open for the next move, but it's not going to happen on this building, it's going to happen on the next one."

Notes

For their quick and efficient response to my many requests for essential materials, I am very grateful to the entire office of Frank O. Gehry and Associates. In particular, I would like to thank Edwin Chan for sharing with me so enthusiastically his experiences as Project Designer; Keith Mendenhall and Matt Fineout for answering innumerable questions on the building process; and Joshua White for his photo research. I would also like to express my appreciation to Jenny Augustyn for her patient retyping of the manuscript; and to my family, Claes, Maartje, and Paulus, for their energizing interest and invaluable support. Resounding thanks go to Berta Gehry, who encouraged me when I needed it, and to Frank Gehry, whose conversations with me over a period of six years I cherish.

1.   Jorge Luis Borges, "Tlön, Uqbar, Orbis Tertius," trans. Alastair Reid, in *Ficciones*, ed. Anthony Kerrigan (New York: Grove Press, 1962), p. 34.

2.   Unless otherwise noted, all quotations by Thomas Krens are from interviews with the author on February 7 and 13, 1997.

3.   Alejandro Zaera, "Conversations with Frank O. Gehry," in *El Croquis* (Madrid) 74/75 (1995), pp. 29, 30.

4.   Unless otherwise mentioned, all quotations by Frank O. Gehry are from conversations with the author between July 1990 and June 1997.

5.   Interview with the author.

6. Roland Barthes, "The Death of the Author," in *Image–Music–Text*, trans. and ed. Stephen Heath (New York: Hill and Wang, 1977), p. 148.

7. Barthes, p. 144.

8. Barthes, p. 148.

9. Peter Arnell and Ted Bickford, eds., *Frank Gehry: Buildings and Projects* (New York: Rizzoli, 1985), p. 268.

10. Gehry, quoted in "No, I'm an Architect," Frank Gehry and Peter Arnell: A Conversation," in Arnell and Bickford, eds., *Frank Gehry*, p. xvii.

11. Ibid.

12. Yukio Futagawa, ed., *GA Architect 10: Frank O. Gehry* (Tokyo: A.D.A. Edita, 1993), p. 174.

13. *The Architecture of Frank Gehry* (Minneapolis: Walker Art Center; New York: Rizzoli, 1986), p. 205.

14. Sylvia Lavin, "Building to My House: Rantings of a Mudpie-Maker, Frank O. Gehry," unpublished interview.

15. Charles Baudelaire, *The Painter of Modern Life and Other Essays* (New York: Da Capo Press, 1964), p. 8.

16. Lavin, "Building to My House."

17. Ibid.

18. Robert A.M. Stern, "Frank O. Gehry: Architecture with a Serious Smile," in Futagawa, ed., *GA Architect 10*, p. 9.

19. *The Architecture of Frank Gehry*, pp. 169, 171.

20. Lavin, "Building to My House."

21. Futagawa, ed., *GA Architect 10*, p. 174.

22. Unpublished transcript of conversation between Gehry and Daniel Buren.

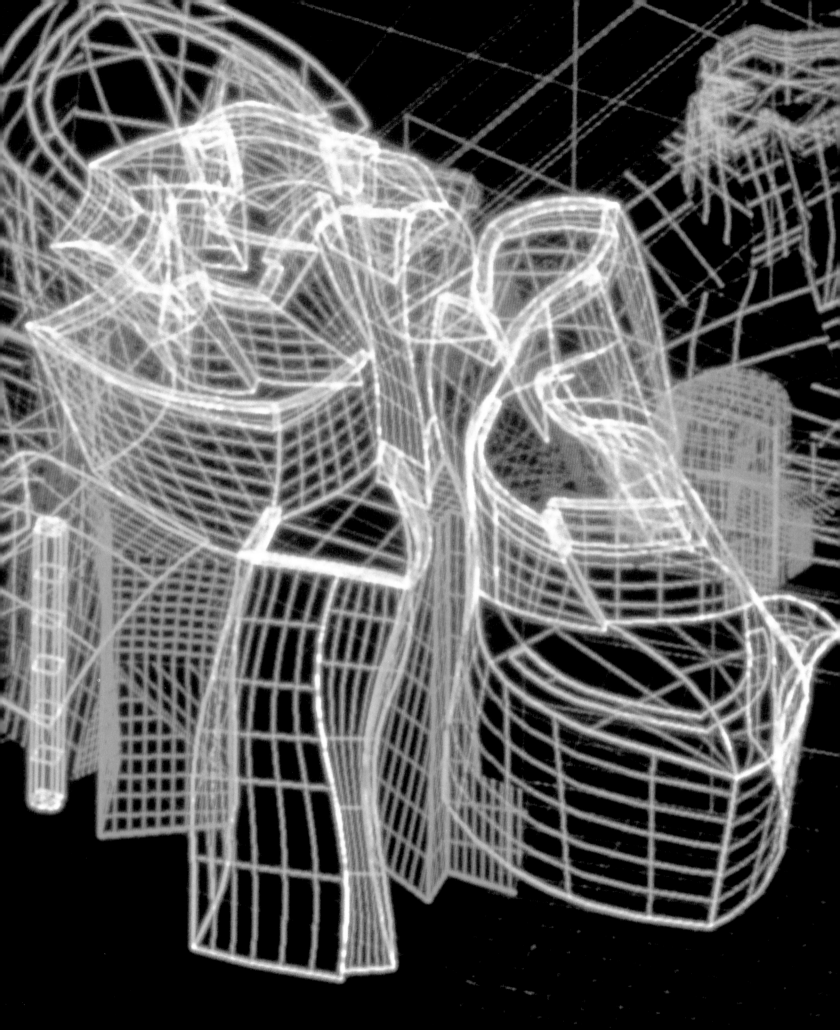

Guggenheim Museum Bilbao,
Catia rendering.

Appendix I: On the Use of the Computer

The Guggenheim Museum Bilbao would not have stayed within the construction budget allotted by the Basque Administration had it not been for Catia, a computer program originally developed for the French aerospace industry, which facilitated the execution process by saving time and preventing inaccurate application of materials. Comprising different packages of software, among others a modeler of architectural faces and volumes, and a definer of the paths used by milling machines in the construction process, Catia had become the program of choice of Jim Glymph, a principal of Frank O. Gehry and Associates. In trying to translate into a structure Gehry's design of a large-scale fish sculpture for the Villa Olímpica complex (1989–92) in Barcelona, Glymph had first looked into different possibilities other architects were exploring at the time; however, these programs, as he saw it, merely "array points in space and then there are massive holes in between.... But Catia, a program that deals with polynomial equations instead of polygons, is pretty much capable of defining any surface as an equation, which means that if you query the computer for any point on that surface, it knows it.... I had to come up with a method of cladding with one panel type that had to be able to change shape. That panel, shaped like an accordion, could then be predetermined in the computer.... We could lay the panels on and build backward, so we built from the outside in and by accident followed the same procedure as an aerospace designer does." And, most importantly, many manufacturers and contractors provided with such information could realize the job more cheaply, with greater accuracy, and in a shorter period of time.

In working with the Catia program, Glymph began to realize that he was dealing with "the most infinitely shapable technology we've ever been presented with," and that in order to follow Gehry's methods and not alter his design process he would have to adopt this technology accordingly, more or less in the tradition of the American creator/inventor working from his backyard garage: "We use software that is pretty much out of the box, although we have some guys down there who customize it, but our application of it is unique, it's ad hoc.

We don't have the kind of budget that the aerospace industry has, so we invent the software as we go.... It is a tool that we could throw away next year if there's another option that would do it better."

Initially, Gehry was resistant to using the computer in his design process. The program seemed to limit architecture to symmetries, mirror imagery, and "simple Euclidean geometries," as Glymph put it, but questions of how to visualize gestural moves resulting in sculptural three-dimensional forms while retaining the immediacy of a sketch, or how to translate them into a very large scale, were unresolved. "I just didn't like the images of the computer," Gehry said, "but as soon as I found a way to use it to build, then I connected." Glymph recalled saying, "Let's clueg together pieces of the equipment to improve the process." He also remembers how he and his team had to hide the machines in a corner, because Gehry did not want to see them: "First we were losing it, but we developed a process through digitizing and visualization on the screen, and a number of other things, where we started to capture the physical mode. And unlike everybody else, we always went back to the physical model."

Until then, Gehry had been frustrated with contractors or manufacturers he consulted who claimed that his sculptural shapes could not be built or were not economical. In acknowledging that their limitations became his own he began to lean more and more toward Frank Lloyd Wright's theory that an architect has to be a master builder as well. A change had taken place in the office, first with the arrival of Glymph, and then the architects Randy Jefferson and Vano Haritunians, as respectively Principal and Associate Principal, to manage projects and break the pattern of having to rely on outsiders. In making use of the new computer program, the layout process was accelerated and, as sculptural shapes could be computed, a more time-saving, economic way of building was devised, affecting, for instance, the structuring of a steel frame, or figuring out what it takes to fit panels together on a wall. The new process could work for both high technology in terms of construction, such as numerically

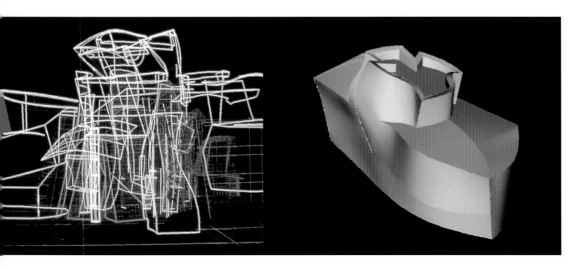

above and facing page: Guggenheim Museum Bilbao, Catia renderings.

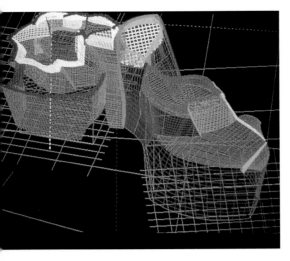

Guggenheim Museum Bilbao,
Catia rendering.

controlled machines, and traditional craft equally well, as demonstrated in the Nationale-Nederlanden office building in Prague, where many full-scale templates were used to design shapes. "Frank Gehry is a big fan of Baroque architecture," said Glymph, "and if you look at the Walt Disney Concert Hall or Bilbao or Prague, what makes any of those projects possible, part of it is their economics."

In order to allow Gehry more freedom in his designing of sculptural shapes, Glymph and his team began analyzing from a technical viewpoint how realizable the forms were while also comparing cost efficiency in terms of volume, surface, and structure: "We could refine a little bit based on those kind of criteria, put them back in front of Gehry as a physical model, so he could again deal with the slightly altered shapes as a thought…and as a gesture." While the designs were brought closer to their immediate realization, Gehry became aware of the computer's power to generate form. Randy Jefferson and Jim Glymph stated in a 1995 interview: "Many of the forms he is developing now are only possible through the computer. Bilbao is a perfect example. Prior to the development of the computer applications in the office, they would have been considered something to move away from. It might have been a sketch idea, but we would never be able to build it. Bilbao could have been drawn with a pencil and straight-edge, but it would take us decades."[1] To Gehry, these ideas have contributed to an irrefutable change in his way of practicing architecture: "We found early in our explorations of developing relations with builders that the more precise the delineation, the more it could be demystified and reduced to the ordering of materials of a certain shape and almost the ability for the contractor to paint by the numbers. It gave the contractors security in their bid and prevented inordinate premiums. Of course it was more expensive but not outrageously so. It is this new process that was first tried on a large scale in Bilbao. It has resulted in a completed building within a reasonable budget, and within a reasonable space of time. What it all leads to, is the architect eventually taking more responsibility and becoming once more the master builder."

1.   Alejandro Zaera, "Conversations with Frank O. Gehry," in *El Croquis* (Madrid) 74/75 (1995), p. 153.

The Guggenheim Museum
Bilbao during construction.

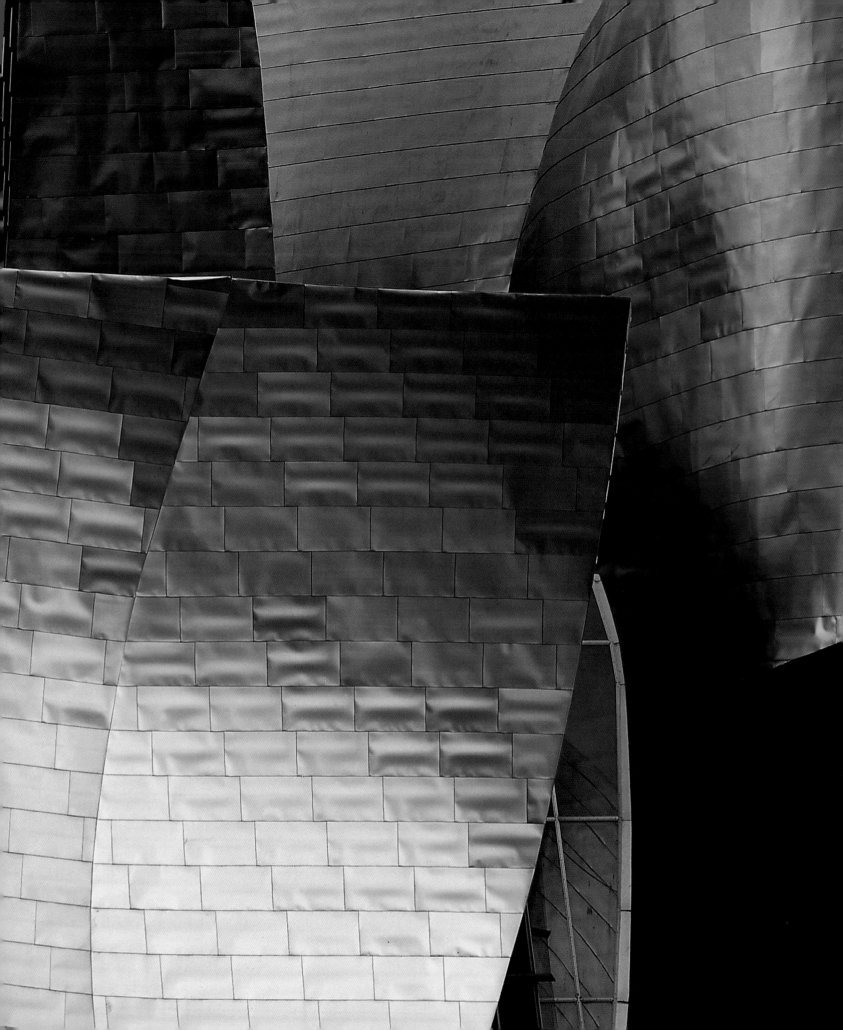

Appendix II: Gehry on Titanium

"The only new material we used in Bilbao was the titanium. The titanium was a replacement for lead copper. We originally planned to use lead copper but it was outlawed as a toxic material. We had to find another material that could play with the light like the lead copper did; it took a long time. We analyzed stainless steel, we put coatings on it, we scratched, rubbed, and buffed it, we tried to take away the cold industrial look of the material, and tried to get a material that was more accessible. It was during that frustration that we found some samples of titanium and looking at it in the light we realized that there was some potential for a metal that had warmth and character. In the initial analysis we found that the titanium was much more expensive than the steel, and might not even be possible to use; so we had to work in two directions at once in case the titanium couldn't be financially viable. Titanium at this point had rarely been used as an exterior material for buildings. It was used as castings for airplane parts, golf clubs, and many other things where strength is a factor. Mined in Russia and Australia, it still has to be rolled and developed for industry near places of large power sources like the Boulder Dam. The rolling of the material, we found, was very delicate. It can lead to a dead surface or a wonderful light-receptive one. And it was difficult for us to determine the method of getting to the one we wanted. In the end, we went back to Pittsburgh, where the rolling took place and watched the material on the assembly line. We asked the fabricator to continue to search for the right mix of oil, acids, rollers, and heat to arrive at the material we wanted. I believe a year of exploration was required to get to where we now are. The titanium is thinner than stainless steel would have been; it is a third of a millimeter thick and it is pillowy, it doesn't lie flat and a strong wind makes its surface flutter. These are all characteristics we ended up exploiting in the use of the material on the building. It's ironic that the stability given by stone is false, because stone deteriorates in the pollution of our cities whereas a third of a millimeter of titanium is a hundred-year guarantee against city pollution. We have to rethink what represents stability."

Titanium skin on the museum's exterior.

Model in basswood and paper submitted to the design competition for the
Guggenheim Museum Bilbao in July 1991.

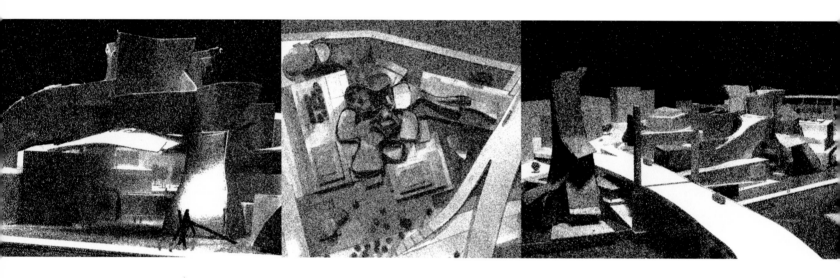

left: Presentation model in plaster and metal shown to the Solomon R. Guggenheim
Foundation's Board of Trustees and Basque officials in New York, September 16, 1991.

right: Section, September 1991.

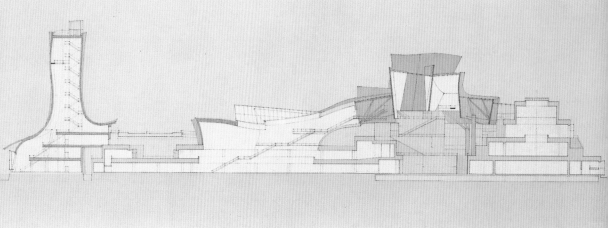

left: Schematic design model in wood and metal, completed in February 1993.

right: Section, February 1993.

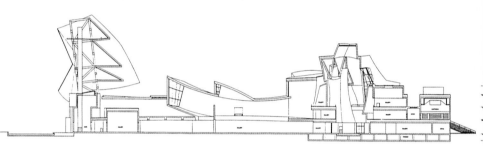

left and center: Schematic design model in wood and paper shown at the ground-breaking of the museum on October 20, 1993.

right: Entrance to the museum during construction, July 1997.

left: Catia rendering.

right: Design model made in basswood and paper, worked on from fall 1992 to December 1993.

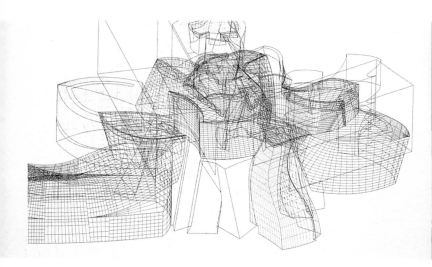

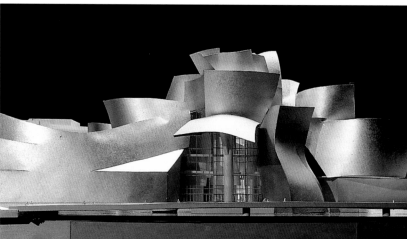

left and right: Verification model in foam and wood made in February 1994.

center: Catia rendering.

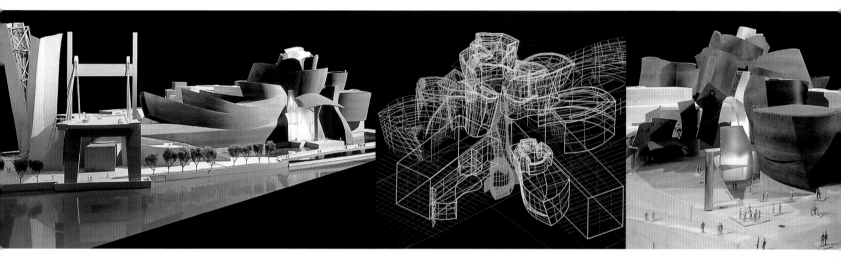

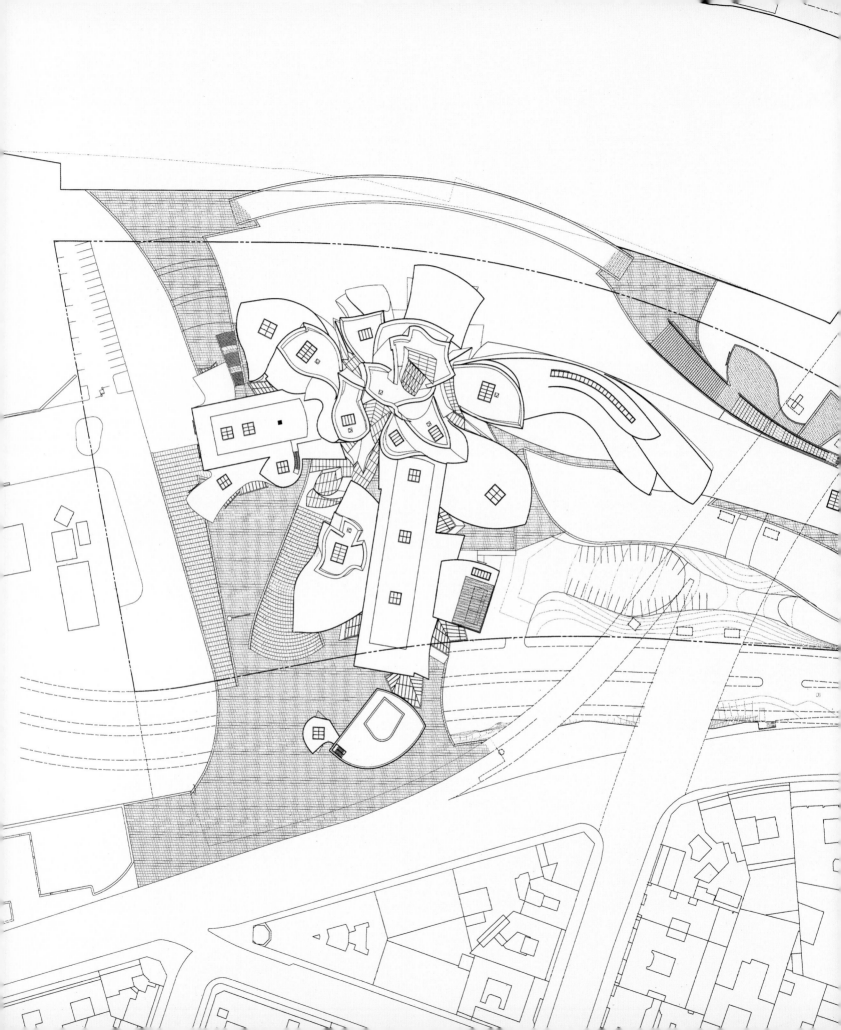

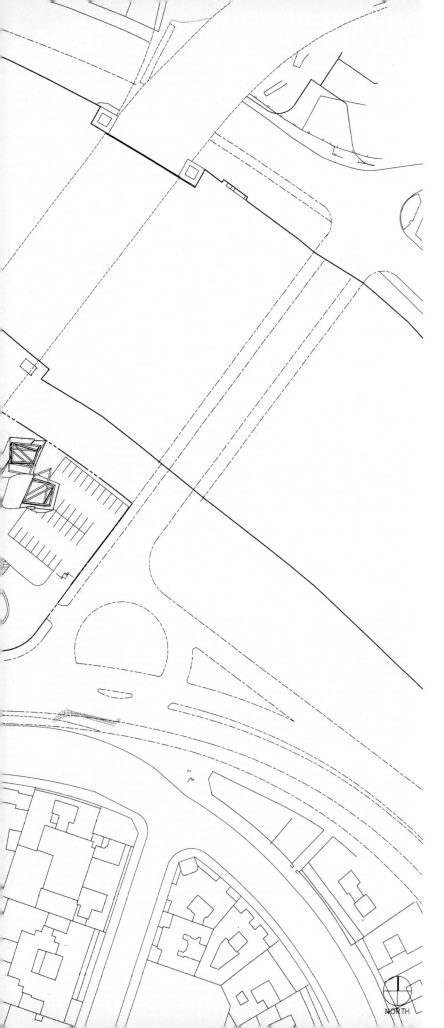

Final site plan.

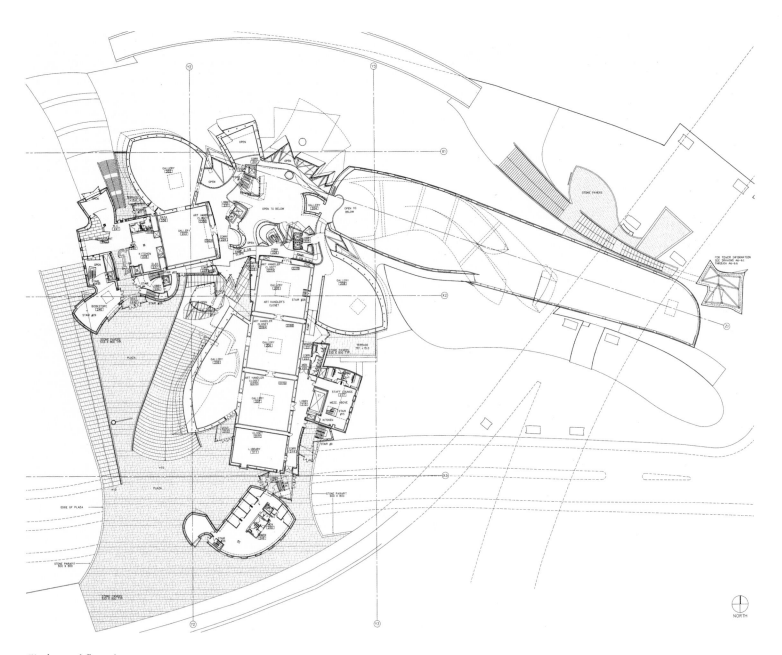

Final second-floor plan.

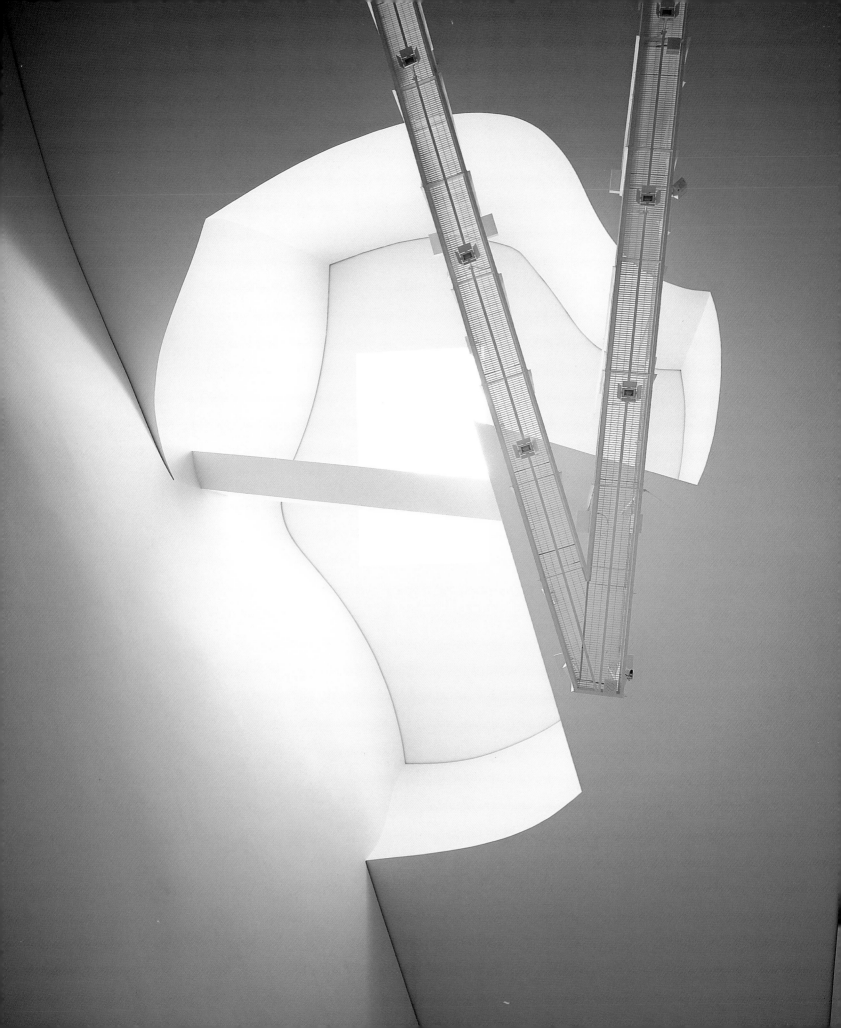

Guggenheim Museum Bilbao

Avenida Abandoibarra, 2
48001 Bilbao
Spain

Architect Frank O. Gehry and Associates, Inc.

Ownership and administration The Guggenheim Museum Bilbao is financed and owned by the Basque administration and is managed by the Guggenheim Museum Bilbao Foundation, an organization that includes representatives of the Basque administration and the Solomon R. Guggenheim Foundation.

Project dates Groundbreaking: October 22, 1993
Public opening: October 19, 1997

Building materials Titanium, Spanish limestone, glass

Project dimensions Site: 32,700 m^2
Gross building area: 28,000 m^2
Building: 24,290 m^2
Galleries: 10,560 m^2
Public space: 2,500 m^2
Library: 200 m^2
Auditorium: 605 m^2
Offices: 1,200 m^2
Museum Store: 375 m^2
Restaurant: 460 m^2
Café: 150 m^2

Project Team

Frank O. Gehry *Design Principal*
Randy Jefferson *Project Principal*
Vano Haritunians *Project Manager*
Douglas Hanson *Project Architect*
Edwin Chan *Project Designer*

Team members

Bob Hale
Rich Barrett
Karl Blette
Tomaso Bradshaw
Matt Fineout
David Hardie
Michael Hootman
Grzegotz Kosmal
Naomi Langer
Mehran Mashayekh
Chris Mercier
Brent Miller
David Reddy
Marc Salette
Bruce Shepard
Rick Smith
Eva Sobesky
Derek Soltes
Todd Spiegel
Jeff Wauer
Kristin Woehl

Executive Architect/Engineer

IDOM (Bilbao)

José Maria Asumendi *Project Director*
Luis Rodriguez Llopis *Project Manager*
César Caicoya *Senior Architect*
Jorge Garay
Javier Ruiz de Prada
Javier Mendieta
Antón Amann
Cruz Lacoma
Amando Castroviejo
José Manuel Uribarri
Rogelio Díez
Ina Moliero
Fernando Pérez Fraile
Pedro Mendarozketa
Miguel Rodriguez
David Prósper
Javier Aróstegui
Victor Zorriqueta
Juan José Bermejo
Fernando Sánchez
Javier Aja
Juan Jesús Garcia
Alvaro Rey
Armando Bilbao
Gonzalo Ahumada
Javier Dávila
Imanol Múgica
Rafael Pérez Borao
Juncal Aldamizechevarría

Consultants

Architectural consultant	Carlos Iturriaga
Solomon R. Guggenheim Foundation representatives	Thomas Hut Andy Klemmer
Structural engineers	Skidmore, Owings and Merrill, Chicago Hal Iyangar *Senior Structural Consultant* John Zils *Associate Partner* Bob Sinn *Project Engineer*
Mechanical engineers	Cosentini Associates, New York Marvin Mass *Partner* Igor Bienstock *Project Engineer* Tony Cirillo *Plumbing/Fire Protection* Edward Martinez *Electrical Engineer*
Lighting	Lam Partners, Boston
Acoustics and audio/visual	McKay, Connant, Brook, Inc., Los Angeles Ernesto Garcia Vadillo
Theater	Peter George Associates, New York
Security	Roberto Bergamo E.A., Italy
Curtain wall	Peter Muller Inc., Houston
Elevator	Hesselberg Keese and Associates, Mission Viejo

Contractors

Foundations	Cimentaciones Abando
Steel and concrete structure	Ferrovial/Lauki/Urssa
External building	Construcciones y Promociones Balzola
Interiors and building systems	Ferrovial
Site works	Ferrovial

Cespa
Agrupación Moda Bizkaia — Moda Vasca
Giroa
SPRI
Estrategia Empresarial
Masterclin
J.K.R. Mat. De Gas y Calefacción
Stai
Grupo ULMA
Pfizer
Previsora Bilbaína
Autoridad Portuaria de Bilbao
Construcciones Sobrino
Diset
Lifelong Learning, Inc.
Cementos Rezola
El Transbordador de Vizcaya
Grupo Ormazabal
SAP España
Pastelería Arrese gozotegia
FAES
Autopista Vasco-Aragonesa, C.E.S.A.
Barceló Clavel Vascohoteles (BC Hoteles)
Paul Mateu Promotion
L'Oréal Profesional
Composites Gurea
Joyería Isabel Sastre
Freixenet, S.A.
Kemen
Tamoin
Compañía de Bebidas Pepsico
Philips Ibérica, S.A.
Kitto
Zurich U.S.
Mapfre
Mutua Vizcaya Industrial
Stollwerck Ibérica, S.L.
Opening
Grupo Martín Berasategui
BNP Paribas España
Vinos de los Herederos del Marqués
de Riscal
Enoteca el Rincón del Vino
Ofiservice
Hotel Abando
Hotel Carlton

Media Park
Tti, S.A.
Hotel Husa Jardines de Albia
Aurtenetxea, S.A.
Hotel Miró
General Electric I.T. Solutions
Tecnalia Corporación Tecnológica
Legrand
Consorcio de Transportes de Bizkaia
Enterasys Networks
Arcelor
TESA Entry Systems
Iverus Ars Vinum

Excmo. Sr. D. José Antonio Ardanza
Excma. Sra. Dña. Pilar Aresti
Sr. D. Rafael Orbegozo
Sr. D. Plácido Arango
D. Leopoldo Rodés
Sra. Dña. Alicia Koplowitz
Sr. D. Eduardo Becerril
Sr. D. Guillermo Barandiaran
Sr. D. Guillermo Caballero de Luján
Sr. D. Fernando Zugaza
Sr. D. Alfonso Zorrilla de Lequerica
Sr. D. David Alvarez
Sr. D. Mario Fernández
Sra. Dña. Mª de los Angeles Aristrain
Sr. D. José Antonio Isusi
Sr. D. José María Arriola
Sr. D. Daniel de Busturia
Sr. D. Manuel March
Sr. D. José Mª Juncadella
Sr. D. Alejandro Aznar
Sr. D. Federico Lipperheide

Bilbao, July 2, 2002